William Humphrey

Recollections of Scottish Episcopalianism

William Humphrey

Recollections of Scottish Episcopalianism

ISBN/EAN: 9783337217563

Printed in Europe, USA, Canada, Australia, Japan

Cover: Foto ©Lupo / pixelio.de

More available books at **www.hansebooks.com**

RECOLLECTIONS
OF SCOTTISH EPISCOPALIANISM.

WORKS BY FATHER HUMPHREY, S.J.

THE ONE MEDIATOR. New Edition, revised and enlarged. 5s.

THE SACRED SCRIPTURES, OR THE WRITTEN WORD OF GOD. 5s.

THE VICAR OF CHRIST. 12mo. 2s. 6d.

CHRISTIAN MARRIAGE. Cheap Edition. Cloth, 1s.; sewed, 6d.

THE BIBLE AND BELIEF. Cheap Edition, 1s.; sewed, 6d.

DISHONEST CONTROVERSY. 3d.

THE DIVINE TEACHER. A Letter to a Friend. With a Preface in reply to No. 3 of the English Church Defence Tracts, entitled *Papal Infallibility*. Sixth Edition. Cloth, 2s. 6d. Cheap edition, wrapper, 1s.

MARY MAGNIFYING GOD. May Sermons. Seventh Edition. 2s. 6d.

OTHER GOSPELS; or, Lectures on St. Paul's Epistle to the Galatians. Crown 8vo, cloth, 4s.

MR. FITZJAMES STEPHEN AND CARDINAL BELLARMINE. 1s.

THE RELIGIOUS STATE. A Digest of the Doctrine of Suarez, contained in his Treatise, *De Statû Religionis*. Three vols. 8vo, 1,200 pp. £1 10s.

ELEMENTS OF RELIGIOUS LIFE. 5s.

In the Press.

CONSCIENCE AND LAW; or, Principles of Human Conduct. Crown 8vo, cloth extra, 4s. 6d. nett.

RECOLLECTIONS

OF

SCOTTISH EPISCOPALIANISM.

BY

(FATHER) HUMPHREY, (S.J.)

LONDON:
' THOMAS BAKER, 1, SOHO SQUARE.

1896.

SOME months ago I found in a second-hand book-shop two volumes on which I had not set eyes for more than a quarter of a century.

One of these volumes was entitled "*A Digest of the Doctrine of St. Thomas on the Sacraments.* By William Humphrey, Missionary Priest in the Diocese of Brechin."

The other volume was entitled "*A Digest of the Doctrine of St. Thomas on the Incarnation.*" The title-page of this volume did not bear the name of any author. Hereby hangs a tale.

The last sheets of this second volume were passing through the press when I was received into the Catholic Church. I could no longer describe myself on the title-page of it, either as in the first volume, or as "Incumbent of St. Mary Magdalene's, Dundee"—a living which I had ceased to hold. It seemed to me, on the other hand, that it would be singularly unbecoming in one who was then sitting on the benches of the Roman College *in statû pupillari* to be, by giving my name as the author of this volume, posing as a teacher of the British public. The publication of the work was beyond my control, but, by the kindness of the publisher, it was allowed to appear as anonymous. The first copy of it reached me in Rome.

The Preface to my volume on the Sacraments is dated from "St. Mary the Virgin, The Cove, near Aberdeen, N.B., Lent, 1867." This book was written among the fisher-folk.

The Cove is a fishing village on the rock-bound coast of Kincardineshire, four miles south of Aberdeen. It is one of a long line of fishing villages which fringe the north-eastern coast of Scotland, a coast which is washed by the German Ocean. The salt sea rolls between it and the coasts of Scandinavia, and the fishers are for the most part sprung from Scandinavian ancestors. Their surnames, which are few in number, are, like my own,

B

which is not a Scottish name, of Scandinavian origin. They were a charming people, those fisher-folk, amongst whom I lived and laboured as a parson for three years, dividing my time between my intercourse with them, and my study of the *Summa* of St. Thomas. Along with no small amount of superstition there lingered among the fishers some traditional traces of the Catholic religion, of even the rudimentary elements of which they had scarcely any knowledge. As an instance, I remember that, when going with a large company of fishermen to the burial of one of their community, all the men, on coming to a ruined bridge by the sea-shore, took off their hats. I asked the reason, but this they could not tell me. " It had always been the custom," they said. One man thought it was because a mermaid had once been seen there. I found out afterwards that on that bridge there had stood in old Catholic days a statue, if not a chapel, of our Lady. The fishers were also most particular in taking utmost care that their dead should be laid out lying due east and west, whatever inconvenience this might cause in their narrow cottages. A lighted candle was always placed beside the corpse, while a plate of salt was laid upon its breast. This was a survival of the old significance of salt as symbolizing the resurrection of the body, but the only reason that the fishers could give me was that it was good for preventing the body swelling. A well, which was still called a saint's well, existed in the neighbourhood, and the bushes round it were strewed with fragments of cloth, while at the bottom of the well itself there always lay pins, and sometimes pieces of money. The forefathers of the fishers had made offerings at the place where they had received benefits through the intercession of the saint. Their descendants, disinherited of the faith of their ancestors, thought only that it was not lucky to pass the well without leaving something in or near it, however small, if only that something belonged to them. When coins were left, they were intended for the benefit of the next beggar who should pass that way. There was no fear of any fisherman abstracting the money that he saw lying at the bottom of the well. The fishers were not beggars, and both fear and pride would have prevented them from appropriating that which they regarded as the property of the poor. The word *sacrilege* was unknown to them, and would have had for them no meaning, but there lingered within their minds the shadow of the idea which that word expresses.

The Cove was situated on the verge of that long, bleak, and barren moor of Drumthwacket, the name of which is familiar to all readers of Sir Walter Scott's *Legend of Montrose*, as the estate of Captain Dugald Dalgetty. Dugald describes it as the "fair patrimony" of his family of four hundred years standing, on account of which he derived his "gentle bluid and designation of Drumthwacket,"—"the Land of Promise, *mea paupera regna*, as we said at Mareschall College,—that place of learning in Aberdeen, the ancient town of Bon Accord," where, he tells us, he had been "imbued with humane letters in his early youth," and had also studied "logical ratiocination," and been taught that *fides et fiducia sunt relativa*.

The Marischal College of Aberdeen, where the soldier of fortune had studied his humanities, and his "natural hereditament of Drumthwacket, that fertile and pleasant spot," as it appeared to him in the vista of long past years, were both of them well known to me. I, too, had studied my humanities at the same Marischal College of Aberdeen, and there, too, I had begun my studies in Scots Law, which I found afterwards of no small service in the study of St. Thomas.

In my day there were not merely two Colleges, but two Universities in Aberdeen, both of which had power to grant degrees. King's College and University was a Papal foundation of the fifteenth century. Marischal College and University had been created by an Earl Marischal in later days, and out of the spoils of the property of the Catholic Church.

The students of both Universities wore scarlet gowns, but we of Marischal College were distinguished from the students of King's by the addition of a broad collar of crimson velvet which lay upon the shoulder. The two Colleges have since been amalgamated in one University.

The town, or rather city of Aberdeen—a designation to its right to which it had two titles, both as having been the see of a Bishop and as being the seat of a University—is of some antiquity. It was the Devana of the Romans. Aberdeen has always been regarded more as a place of learning than as a centre of commerce, or a town of trade, and in the city the learned professions of divinity, law, and medicine abounded. The Established Church in Aberdeen was of course, as elsewhere in Scotland, Presbyterian, but side by side with it and other forms of Presbyterianism there existed both in town and country a large body of Episcopalians, and a not inconsiderable number of Roman Catholics. Of the Episcopalians there were two distinct bodies. One was called the Scottish Episcopal Church, which was autonomous, and governed by its own Bishops. The other consisted of a number of " English chapels." These used the Book of Common Prayer of the Church of England, and were ministered to by clergymen in English Orders, but they were not subject to any Bishop. Their children were usually sent for Confirmation to the Bishop of Carlisle, although that prelate did not pretend any jurisdiction over them, nor did they regard him as their diocesan. He was simply the nearest Bishop from whom they could receive the rite of Confirmation, since they were disowned by the Bishops of the Scottish Episcopal Church, with which they were not in ecclesiastical communion. The origin of those " English chapels " was political rather than religious. The members of them were adherents of the House of Hanover, took the oaths to Government, and offered public prayers for the reigning royal family. They were therefore tolerated.

The Scottish Episcopalians, on the other hand, were for the most part Jacobite in their political leanings, held the House of Stuart in unbounded veneration, and would not for the world offer public prayers for the House of Hanover. They were in consequence proscribed by Government. This gave rise to the existence of the English chapels. The difference between the two bodies, so far as religious belief is concerned, was not greater than is the difference which exists between the various parties which compose the Church of England. Broadly speaking, the English chapels were Evangelical or Low Church, while the Scottish Episcopalians were nearly all of them more or less High Church. As a body their strong point was Baptismal Regeneration. They believed also, to some extent at least, in the sacramental efficacy of Confirmation, of Orders, and of Matrimony. The Sacrament of Penance was among them practically in abeyance, although among the older members there were whispered tales of exceptional instances of the practice not only of auricular confession, but even of Extreme Unction. Their belief with regard to the Eucharist was very much the same as that of the Caroline divines. They resembled in sentiment the Nonjurors, and were in sympathy with the earlier Tractarians, with this exception in their own favour that they claimed to have always held that which the Tractarians had but recently discovered. The favourite motto of the Scottish Episcopalians was—" Evangelic Truth, and Apostolic Order." By this they practically meant the three-fold ministry of Bishops, Priests, and Deacons, with a doctrinal position which was at once equally removed from Rome, on the one hand, and from Geneva, on the other.

In the celebration of the Eucharist there were two liturgical rites in use among them. Some congregations followed the English Book of Common Prayer, while other congregations not a few made use of the rite which went by the name of the Scottish Communion Office. This was framed on the model of the Liturgy of St. James, and of other early Eastern Liturgies. It contained an Invocation of the Holy Ghost after the words of consecration, and until this had been made, the consecration was not supposed to have taken place.

The use of either of those two formularies was to a great extent optional, or determined by circumstances or custom. Some, especially of the older congregations, preferred the Scottish Office both as being a national rite, and as linking them, in sentiment at least, with the "unchanging East," of which, however, they knew next to nothing. Others, and among them many of the High Churchmen of the modern type, preferred the English Communion Service as being more in unison with the Roman rite, and with the other liturgies of Western Christendom.

When I lived in Aberdeen some five-and-thirty years ago the Scottish Episcopal Church was in the throes of an intestine controversy on the subject of the Eucharist. It arose in this way. The Protestant Bishop of Brechin, Dr. Alexander Penrose Forbes, in a Charge to the clergy of his diocese, in the autumn of 1857, propounded a real and objective presence of the true Body and Blood of Christ in the Eucharist, in terms which more nearly approached the Catholic doctrine than does the ordinary language of Protestant divines. For this he was delated to the Episcopal Synod as a teacher of unsound doctrine, and he was tried by his fellow-Bishops. At the trial Dr. Forbes pleaded that the opinions which he held were not such as to subject him to penal consequences, and on this point he gained his case, and was let off with an admonition to be more careful in his pronouncements for the future. The Rev. Patrick Cheyne, of St. John's Church, Aberdeen, an advanced High Churchman, had also set forth his views on the Eucharist in a course of six sermons, which he preached during the Lent of 1857, and published in the following year. Mr. Cheyne maintained that the incriminated doctrines were not mere permissible opinions which might be held and taught within the limits of his Church without fear of penal consequences, but that they were revealed doctrines of the Catholic faith which could not without heresy be denied, and consequently that either they were doctrines of his Church, or that that Church was heretical. For this Mr. Cheyne was impeached and tried, found guilty and suspended. He then denounced his accusers and judges as heretics, and for this he was deposed from the ministry of the Scottish Episcopal Church.

Mr. Thomson, of Banchory, a pious Presbyterian country gentleman of fair estate not far from Aberdeen, universally respected and even revered throughout the county, in a pamphlet which he published with the title of *Scottish Episcopacy, Past and Present,* and which was "reprinted at the request of the Church Protestant Defence Society," in 1860, says : "The present state of the Scottish Episcopal Church, small as it is, is most deplorable ; and, but for its lofty pretensions, would excite the liveliest pity of all who see it. It has ever held up *unity* as the perfection of a Church ; and in one sense with truth, when the unity is that of Scripture, viz., living union with Christ the Living Head—apart from all forms and ceremonies and questions of government. But it long enjoyed its unity all to itself. It was united in this manner to no other body of Christians, and now even this unity has vanished, and it is torn asunder by irreconcileably opposed doctrines on the subject of the Eucharist. The Bishop in Aberdeen has tried and deposed one of his presbyters for holding and teaching doctrines considered to be equivalent to the Transubstantiation of Rome. We regard Mr. Cheyne's doctrines as wholly un-Scriptural, and therefore heretical ; but we also believe that they are the very essential doctrines of his own Church, as proved by her Communion Service *of primary authority,* and therefore we think Mr. Cheyne has had cause to complain of the treatment he has received. He was well entitled to plead : 'If I am wrong, our whole Church is in the wrong, and you, my judges, are all in the wrong also. If, therefore, you think me wrong, then begin by reforming the Church to which we all belong. Expunge from its service those doctrines which you now condemn, and which I am teaching, because I believe them, and have found them in our acknowledged standards—give up, avowedly, those peculiar doctrines for which our Church has contended from the days of Laud even to our own; form a new Church with new Offices, and then I will tell you whether I can conscientiously go along with you or not; but do not condemn me for having hitherto fully preached the doctrines to which you all have, like me, subscribed as the very doctrines which you hold. Do not condemn in *me* what you uphold in our Communion Service by your solemn subscriptions.'

"Mr. Cheyne is now deposed, and his successor has been instituted. This moment has been chosen by the High Church party in the Church of England to present to Mr. Cheyne an address of sympathy and condolence, signed, as stated in the newspapers of the day, by 358 clergymen and 3,942 lay-members of the Church of England. It is startling to find that so many clergymen of the Church of England hold opinions diametrically opposed to the Articles they have signed as the Articles of their faith; but it is well for the Church of England that they have thus made themselves known.

"Another, and a more important case, as displaying the principles and practices of the Scottish Episcopal Church, arose immediately out of that of Mr. Cheyne. One of her Bishops, who had taken an active part in defending Mr. Cheyne when on his trial, was himself accused by one of his own clergy of holding opinions similar to those of Mr. Cheyne, or perhaps which tended still more decidedly towards Romanism, and has been publicly tried by his peers, the other Bishops of his Church. This proceeding was so novel that, like Mr. Cheyne's, the case while in progress excited great curiosity on the part of the public. The results, however, in the two have been widely different. Mr. Cheyne was suspended and virtually deposed, while the Bishop escapes all punishment save a very peculiar admonition. The only perceptible difference betwixt the two cases seems to lie in this, that while both the accused held the self-same doctrines, the Bishop in his defence made certain dialectic definitions and distinctions, in no way affecting the essence of his doctrines, but only clothing them in an impenetrable robe of obscurity, while Mr. Cheyne vouchsafed no comments, but simply adhered to his opinion.

"We may be mistaken, but we cannot see any real Scriptural difference betwixt the doctrine of Bishop Forbes and that of Mr. Cheyne. We think both erroneous, and both at the same time strictly in conformity with the Communion Office and catechisms of the Scottish Episcopal Church; but the Synod has not ventured to condemn in the Bishop what they had previously condemned in the presbyter.

"Perhaps the action of the Bishops may have been restrained by their knowledge of the singular esteem in which Bishop Forbes's personal character and untiring benevolence are justly held, not only by his own flock, but also by those who have no sympathy with his High Church doctrines; and yet the same feeling of personal esteem was as applicable to Mr. Cheyne in his more limited sphere of action. To a mere spectator, the difference seems very strange. Can it be that their relative positions in their Church had any influence in the matter? A *presbyter*, however pure and exemplary in his life, might be suspended for erroneous doctrine without much danger; but a *Bishop!* he must not be troubled beyond a certain point, lest damage should ensue to the order.

"What appears to be the most remarkable characteristic of the proceedings of the Synod is the difficulty, or rather impossibility, of attaching any distinct meaning to the various speeches of the Bishops, or even to the embodiment of their opinions in their sentence. Bishop Terrot, Bishop Wordsworth, and Bishop Eden delivered their judgments at great length, yet giving no *understandable* opinions on the greater part of the questions at issue, but on the whole rather excusing the Bishop. Thus Bishop Eden, while objecting to the words used by Bishop Forbes to explain his views as to the presence of our Redeemer in the Eucharist, adds: 'He believed that the proposition of the Bishop of Brechin was cleared by his theory of a superhuman, supra-local, hyper-physical body, from direct identity with the Sacrifice of the Mass, in connection with his explanation that he meant only a passive and not an active Sacrifice!' Bishops Ewing, Suther, and Wilson contented themselves with expressing concurrence in the opinions of their brethren. The tendency of the whole speeches, as reported, seems to show a wish to find fault with Bishop Forbes for his frank avowal of his opinions, rather than to condemn the opinions themselves. With these there is throughout a lurking sympathy, which prevents the Bishops from giving a clear and unmistakeable decision.

"The practical conclusion, however, as contained in the latter part of the sentence, is really a very suitable termination to the whole mass of confusion: 'But in consideration of the explanations and modifications offered by the respondent in his answers, in reference to the first charge, and in consideration also that the respondent now only asks toleration for his opinions, but does not claim for them the authority of the Church, or any right to enforce them on those subject to his jurisdiction, we, the said College of Bishops, feel that we best discharge our duty in this painful case by limiting our sentence to a declaration of censure and admonition ; and we do now solemnly admonish, and in all brotherly love entreat, the Bishop of Brechin to be more careful for the future, so that no fresh occasion may be given for trouble and offence, such as have arisen from the delivery and publication of the primary charge to the clergy complained of in the Presentment. And we declare the proceedings in this case to be now concluded.'

"By this most lame conclusion, Bishop Forbes is left at perfect liberty to teach his own doctrines, providing he teaches them merely as his own opinions, so long as he does not enforce them as those of his Church. Surely his brother Bishops, by announcing this conclusion, condemn themselves as either very indifferent as to whether truth or error be taught, or as wholly unable to find out and say what is truth in the matter, or even to tell their people what their own Church holds and believes to be the truth.

"A Presbyterian may, perhaps, not be reckoned a very good judge of the powers and duties of a Bishop of the Scottish Episcopal Church ; but surely the plain meaning of the word επισκοπος, or overseer, in a Church, implies that the important function of a man holding such an office is to take care that his subordinates teach no heresy for truth ; whereas here we have a whole College of Bishops granting leave to a *brother Bishop* to teach his people what they have condemned *in a presbyter ;* provided always that the Bishop, when so teaching heresy, takes care to warn his people that it is only his own doctrine and not that of his Church. Why did they not give a similar licence to the presbyter? The Scottish Episcopal Church is now more loudly than ever proclaiming its identity

with the Church of England, and endeavouring to obtain the
sanction of the Legislature to its assertions; and yet its own
clergy and bishops are not at one in regard to one fundamental
doctrine of every Christian Church, viz., the nature of Christ's
Presence in the Eucharist.   Until they can give forth one
certain doctrine on this point, it is vain for them to claim
identity with the clear doctrine of the Thirty-Nine Articles of
the Church of England."

The passages in Mr. Cheyne's sermons on the Holy Eucharist
which he was called upon to retract and apologize for, under
pain of suspension, were :

(1) When having defined the Eucharistic Presence in the
following words and pronounced it to be error to teach otherwise, viz., "when I speak of the Real Presence, I mean, as the
Church means, that after consecration, whole Christ, God and
Man, is really, truly, and substantially present in the Eucharist,
under the form of bread and wine;"—when, having laid down
this definition, he declares that "the Sacrifice of the Eucharist
is substantially the same as the Sacrifice of the Cross, differing
only in the manner of offering."

(2) When he further declares, that in the Lord's Supper "we
kneel to the Lord Himself, invisibly present under the form,"
or "under the veils of bread and wine."

(3) And lastly, when he pronounces that "the only thing
necessary to the completion of the Sacrifice is the Communion
of the priest."

Mr. Cheyne had lost his living, and he had to leave his
beloved St. John's, which had been to him for years the honest
pride of his clerical life, and as the very apple of his eye.   He
had built and beautified it in accordance with what were then
the highest ideals of ritual correctness.   He was succeeded by
the Rev. Frederick George Lee, and by-and-bye the modern
Ritualism was introduced full-blown into the Scottish Episcopal
Church.   This Ritualism was an exotic, and at first found some
difficulty in taking root in soil which, although it had been
sown with the highest of High Church doctrines, had been
cultivated ritually after old-fashioned methods.   I remember
well the first time I saw the Eucharistic vestments, as they were
called, and smelt incense in a Protestant church.   It was at
St. John's, Aberdeen, at a Christmas midnight service.

The congregation of St. John's was divided in opinion with regard to these novel rites, and part swarmed off with Mr. Lee to another church, which however the Bishop refused to license. The new venture turned out a financial failure, and Mr. Lee left Aberdeen. The terms which Dr. Suther, then Protestant Bishop of Aberdeen, exacted from Mr. Lee, as conditions, without complying with which he would neither grant his licence for Mr. Lee's new church nor be present at the opening of it for Divine worship, were : (1) the removal of the crucifix on the rood-beam, the figures of Our Lady and St. John on either side of it, and the inscription which ran beneath it. (2) The removal of the lamp which was suspended before the altar. (3) That everything to be placed, either permanently or temporarily, by way of decoration or furniture, in the chancel, or upon, over, or about the altar or holy table, should be first submitted to the Bishop's inspection and approval. (4) That Mr. Lee should give to the Bishop his word in writing that neither he, his curate, nor any other clergyman with his consent, should use the crypt or mortuary altar for the celebration of the Holy Eucharist. (5) That Mr. Lee should give to the Bishop—who had been informed on undoubted authority that he and his curate, or others assisting him in the service of his church, were in the habit of arraying themselves " in unauthorized vestments," like those worn by clergymen of the Roman Catholic Church—his promise in writing that hereafter, on no occasion, either he, his curate, or any other clergyman assisting at St. Mary's, should use such vestments as copes, chasubles, coloured stoles, other than black, but should wear the vestments ordinarily now in use in this church. (6) That Mr. Lee must give a written promise that incense should not be used again on any occasion in his church. The Bishop concluded his ultimatum with the words—" I feel that I would not be acting the part of a faithful overseer of the Church in this diocese if I did not now put myself on the defensive against these compromising encroachments on our customs ; and I hope that you will not hesitate to accede to these terms, which I, as your Bishop, consider essential, not merely for the sake of your own usefulness, but for preserving the order and uniformity of our Reformed Church."

2.

By this time I had completed my studies in Scots Law at Edinburgh, under Professors Shank More, and Montgomery Bell, and when I was of age I entered the Society of Advocates in Aberdeen, of which my father was a member. My mind was, however, becoming more and more engrossed with Church matters, and at last I definitely resolved to take Orders in the Scottish Episcopal Church. With a view to this I went in the first place to the College of the Holy Ghost in the Isle of Cumbrae. This island is the larger of two small islands opposite Bute and Arran, in the Frith of Clyde. It is recorded of a Presbyterian minister of Cumbrae that he used to pray on Sundays for the welfare of Muckle Cumbrae and Little Cumbrae, and the adjacent islands of Great Britain and Ireland. On the larger of the two islands—some three or four miles long and from a mile to a mile-and-a-half broad—stood the College and Collegiate Church, erected by the Hon. George Boyle, afterwards Earl of Glasgow, a strong High Churchman and disciple of Dr. Pusey. The College was at first intended to be a seminary of students for the ministry of the Scottish Episcopal Church, who should form a semi-monastic body. This scheme, however, fell through, and in my time the College was frequented chiefly by young men of more or less High Church opinions from Oxford, who came there to spend the long vacation and to read with the Vice-Provost. There came also from time to time several High Church clergymen of the Church of England, who were Honorary Canons of Cumbrae. The tone of the place was distinctly High Church, but with great variety of heights and tones and shades of High Churchism. I remember one dignitary who held firmly the real and objective presence of Christ in the Eucharist, but who had fortified himself against the Roman error of Communion under one kind by his ingenious invention of a presence in the Eucharist of the Dead Christ, or of Christ as He was during the three days of His death. Since Christ's Blood was then separated from His Body, he argued the necessity of Communion under both kinds. It is fair, however, to say that his patent heresy did not find popular acceptance.

It was at Cumbrae that I first made the acquaintance of St. Thomas Aquinas. I was introduced to the *Summa* by Dr. Cazenove, the Vice-Provost, with whom I was reading. The worthy Doctor had little conception of the fruit that was to spring from the seed which he was thus the means of sowing.

While at Cumbrae I was strongly advised to take Orders in the Church of England, and not in the Scottish Episcopal Church, on account of the consequences of the Cheyne case. The last remains of political proscription had not passed away. Men in Scottish Orders still lay under legal disabilities, which barred preferment in the Established Church of England, with which, nevertheless, they were ecclesiastically in full communion. It was quite within the range of possibility, and it was even not improbable, that with my doctrinal views I might be suspended or deposed as Mr. Cheyne had been, and that I would in that event be ecclesiastically stranded. If Mr. Cheyne had been in English Orders, instead of being in Scottish Orders, his deposition from the ministry of the Scottish Episcopal Church would not have prevented his obtaining preferment and a wider sphere in the Church of England, through the influence of many English Churchmen who were his devoted admirers, and regarded him as a confessor for the faith. Strange to say, it was this very danger that had for me the strongest attraction. I was determined to throw in my lot with "the suffering remnant," as the Scottish Episcopalian clergy were called, and loved to be called. I was resolved not only to have Scottish Orders, but to prepare for the reception of them by a purely Scottish training. I entered therefore at the College of Glenalmond after my year at Cumbrae—and I took St. Thomas with me.

3.

Trinity College, Glenalmond, at the entrance to the Perthshire highlands, had been founded with a two-fold end in view— as the recognized seminary of the Scottish Episcopalian body for its divinity students—and as a school for the sons of Scotch gentlemen, on the model of the public schools of England. Mr. Gladstone was a prime mover in the foundation of this institution, as may be read in the Life of Mr. Hope Scott, who was excluded from the governing body, on account of his being suspected of Roman leanings. The theological atmosphere at Glenalmond was very different from that of Cumbrae. It was toned to the "comprehensiveness" of the Church of England. One incident will give the character of the common doctrine current at Glenalmond. The subject of the Warden's theological lecture was on one occasion the Eucharist, and he maintained a real and objective presence of the Body and Blood of Christ therein. At question time I asked whether, that being the case, the doctrine of the Church of England is that Divine worship is to be paid as due to the Blessed Sacrament? " By no means," said Dr. Hannah. " The Church of England teaches two truths —the Real Presence of Christ in the Sacrament—and that no adoration is to be given to the Sacrament. She does not endeavour to reconcile these truths; in the sobriety of her doctrine she merely states them. It follows therefore that her teaching is that, while Christ is really present in the Sacrament, He is present in such a way that He is not therein to be adored." This utterance threw some light on the Warden's habitually leaving a litter of crumbs on and about the communion-table after his celebration of the Lord's Supper. A High Church member of the College, who did not hold his chief's views on " Eucharistic Adoration," used to fee the manciple, whose duty it was to sweep the sanctuary, to allow him to collect the crumbs after the service, and " reverently consume " them. The Warden objected also to our being present at the Communion unless we were prepared at the same time to partake. He allowed that " non-communicating attendance " was being practised in the Church of England, and that it might with reason be permitted at Cumbrae, but he would not have any exciting controversy in his College, where he had to provide for all sorts and conditions of men. For those, therefore, who believed in " fasting Communion," and believed also in their obligation to assist at the Sacrifice of the Altar on Sundays, Sundays at Glenalmond were practically fast-days.

For one thing I remain ever grateful to the Warden. He taught us most admirably Aristotle's *Ethics*. The ethics he had at his fingers' ends, and in them he had been a more than successful coach at Oxford. To the Warden I was indebted also for the loan, on condition that I should not show it to any of the other students, of Newman's *Apologia*, which was then coming out in parts.

Meantime I went on with the study of St. Thomas in my own rooms. I found in it nutriment which was as solid and satisfying as it was palateable after the doctrinal sawdust of the lectures on Paley and Pearson.

During the two years that I spent at Glenalmond, I came across Newman's *Essay on Development*, Ward's *Ideal of a*

Christian Church, Wilberforce's *Principles of Church Authority*, and similar works, such as converts in those days were wont to write to inform the British public of the reasons for their submission to the Catholic Church. By the argument of one of those books I was much exercised and shaken. So far as I remember it, or remember the effect that it left on my mind, it came to this, that the Church was first Apostolic—then Episcopal—thereafter Patriarchal—and finally Papal. The Papacy was the Church's practical interpretation of her own constitution. The Roman Pontificate was a necessary outcome by way of *evolution*. There must necessarily be a Bishop of Bishops, if the Universal Church is not to be destitute of a special perfection—in a centre of corporate unity—which belongs to every particular church or diocese. A Papacy thus seemed to me to follow as a necessary conclusion from the principles of Episcopalianism.

I did not then see how entirely erroneous the whole of this theory was, inasmuch as it supposed the Papacy to be the cope-stone instead of being the foundation of that edifice which Christ called His Church, and which He built upon the living Rock of Peter.

I only know this, that I was staggered by what seemed to me to be the cogency of the argument. I forthwith betook myself to the Bishop of Brechin. Dr. Forbes had asked me to come to his diocese. This I was free to do, and he had offered to ordain me. I put the case plainly before him, along with my mortal misgiving that I must, instead of coming to be ordained by him, go away at once and make my submission to the Roman Catholic Church.

The Bishop heard most patiently what I had to say. He then remained for some moments apparently absorbed in thought. He broke the silence by saying slowly, and as if soliloquizing, and following by himself alone the current of his thought—" What a marvellous creation is the Roman Church— so strong at its extremities, and so rotten at its centre." Turning to me, he then said most feelingly : " My dear fellow, they will make you miserable. Instead of escaping from our difficulties, you will land yourself amidst far greater difficulties than any from which we are suffering. You will have to choose your party in the Roman Church. Either you will proclaim yourself a Gallican, and keep your reason—or you will give up your reason and attach yourself to Manning's party.

If you join the Gallicans, you will expose yourself to a relentless persecution. They are in a minority, and the Ultramontanes are at present the dominant party in the Church of Rome. Moreover, and this is what is worse, it is their party that you will as a convert be logically bound to join. It is all very well for hereditary Roman Catholics, who have been born and bred in Gallicanism, to remain in it, but it would be absolutely absurd in you, as a convert to the Church of Rome, to join a party which is barely tolerated in it. A convert's very reason, if he desires to keep his reason, demands that he should surrender it to the dominant party, the spirit of which is at present the real spirit of the Latin Church. We in the Anglican Church have our difficulties, it is true, and no one can feel them more keenly or suffer from them more acutely than I do—our isolation from the rest of Christendom—our disunion amongst ourselves—the toleration in our midst of erroneous or inadequate doctrine—neglect of the Daily Sacrifice, and the like—but, thank God, things are bettering and mending. Our difficulties are not of our own seeking or of our own making. They have fallen to us in our appointed lot. We have inherited them. They surround us in the providence of God, and in the same providence we are called upon to co-operate in the work of the restoration of the Church's unity. You, dear friend, have been captivated by the beauty of a glorious ideal. I cannot give you hope that you will find the ideal that has presented itself to you realized in the Church of Rome. The unity that you imagine, does not exist in the Roman Church.

" Döllinger, their most learned historian and the greatest of their theologians, does not encourage individual secessions to Rome from the Church of England. He said to a common friend of mine and his, a well-known statesman, that there are three classes of English Churchmen who became Roman Catholics. There were the very *intellectual*—men like Newman—men who had, and knew it, along with their intellectuality, a strong strain within them of latent infidelity. Those men felt that if they would keep their faith, they must place themselves under lock and key, and plant their feet against the door of entrance to any doubt. It was an almost necessity for such men to go to Rome.

" There were other Church of England men who were very *materialistic*, men who were carried away by the sensuous attractions of a gorgeous ritual, with splendid vestments and smoking incense, and who found what they sought and longed for in the pomp and pageantry of Roman ceremonial worship.

"There was also a third class of converts composed of High Churchmen, whose character was *concupiscible* rather than irascible, in the sense that they sought to have the *bonum sine arduo*. They wanted the spoils of victory without the conflict—the crown without the cross. These men found ready to their hand in the Church of Rome the spiritual luxuries for which they had to fight and suffer in the Church of England."

In this latter class I seemed to find myself at the end of the Bishop's conversation. He had been most kind and sympathetic. This soothed me. A tone of compassion for what he feared would be my disappointment in the Church of Rome, infected me with a corresponding dread of the possibility of disillusionment. It must be remembered, also, that neither the theory which had fascinated me, nor either my own conception or the Bishop's conception of a Universal Church, rose higher or nearer to the truth than that of a confederation of particular churches or episcopal dioceses, under the presidency of one Bishop of Bishops.

If Dr. Forbes had met me with upbraiding, remonstrance, or argument, I should have had much to say for myself and in defence of ideas which had absorbed my mind, and I might have shown that in my temperament there was rather more of the irascible than of the concupiscible. His clever treatment of me not only disarmed me, but impressed me with a sense of my own ignorance, and with a feeling that I had been standing on the verge of the abyss of a grave imprudence, from the lifelong consequences of which his wisdom had wisely saved me. Dr. Forbes had lived in Rome, and I had never been in Rome, and so had no judgment of my own to oppose to his, with regard to the "rottenness at its centre" of the Roman Catholic Church. The Bishop had intimate friends, and these not a few, both among the Gallicans and in "Manning's party," while I had not even chance acquaintances in either set. I could not, therefore, check his statements. He was confident of the validity of his Orders. With regard to jurisdiction, he said that it was a vexed question, about which even Roman canonists were in disagreement. If I must "go over," he told me, I should go with his best blessing, and he would ever follow my career with

c

heartfelt wishes for my happiness and welfare. He could never, however, cease to deplore that I had made myself a Roman Catholic on the most Protestant of principles—by a deliberate exercise of my own private judgment.

If, on the other hand, I should remain where Providence had placed me, to do the work which Providence had set before me, I should be in any case undoubtedly a priest, and so long as I continued praying daily and offering the Sacrifice of the Altar, and labouring by word and deed for the reunion of the sees of Scotland and of England with the central See of Christendom, I could not possibly be *formally* schismatic, even if, on the almost incredible hypothesis, it should turn out that those sees were *materially* in schism.

I did remain in the Anglican communion, and I still think that with my then views I was sincere and justified in so remaining.

The Bishop did his best to ordain me, and by-and-bye I found myself stationed at The Cove.

4.

I had taken St. Thomas with me. Without St. Thomas I do not know what I should have done. The *Summa* was my daily bread. It was always lying open on the table before me, and when I looked up from its pages, there lay before me the German Ocean. The outlook from my study was like that from the stern of a ship that is homeward bound, in this, that from the window I saw no land, but only the sea before me. There were always ships and steamers passing by, and sometimes the sea was studded with a fleet of fishing-boats. Whenever these went out, I used to betake myself to the cliffs, which were crowded with the wives and mothers and daughters and sisters of the fishermen. In foul weather they and I met again upon the cliffs. I said nothing, but the women felt that I felt with them. Again we were together on the cliffs when the fishing-boats came in. On sea the fishermen were themselves and quitted themselves like the manly, sturdy, and self-reliant men they were. On the instant that their boats touched ground the men were abject in their subjection to their womankind. The fisherwomen and the fisher-girls waded through the surf, and took possession of the fishing-boats and of all that the boats contained. The men went straightway home, to refresh their wearied bodies and to make up their arrears of well-earned sleep. On land the fisherwomen reigned supreme over every fisherman, whether husband, or son, or brother, or father. The fish found in the boats they regarded as their own unquestioned and unquestionable property, and with their administration they would brook no interference. The fishermen might form a House of Lords on sea, but the fisherwomen constituted on land a House of Commons, and in their hands were held the purse-strings. Those strong, sturdy women carried the fish upon their backs in *creels*, or large baskets of wicker-work, to Aberdeen—a distance of four miles—for sale. All the fisher-wives were dressed alike in short petticoats of blue stuff, with wrappers or bodices of the same or other material, and with *mutches*, or caps of well-starched linen, not unfrequently edged with lace. This was their uniform, and it had been the uniform of their ancestresses for generations. In it they looked picturesque. Without it they would have looked sordid and loathsome. The physical strength of those fisherwomen was extraordinary. I have known a fisherwoman, three or four days after her con-finement, carry on her back, a distance of four miles into Aberdeen, a *creel* of fish which her husband could scarcely lift. The chastity of the fisherwomen was almost perfect. The fishermen were for the most part chaste, but they were not immaculate. When they failed, it was not in their intercourse with the fisherwomen at any rate of their own village. This would have been "working folly in Israel." Their occasional misdemeanours were generally with the inland women, who were not of their race. Even then, if a fisherman had got a country woman into trouble, he was held bound by the fisher code of honour to marry her, and so make her what they called an "honest woman." The honest woman had, nevertheless, for the future an evil time. Never, to the day of her death, was her past forgotten by the fisherwomen, nor did they permit her to forget it.

Not far from The Cove was the fishing-village of Finnan, or Findon, from which the smoked haddocks, which the railways have now brought even to English breakfast-tables, take their name of "Finnan Haddies." The curing of them was not confined to Findon, but was practised at The Cove as well as in the other villages along the coast. The process was this. The haddocks were split open, gutted, flattened out, and rubbed with salt. Smouldering peats were laid on the earthen floor in a corner of the cottage, and on these was sprinkled wet sawdust. This produced a thin bluish-grey smoke, the odour of which was penetrating, but not unpleasant to those who had become accustomed to it. Over this the haddocks were hung on a *hake*. The hake was a triangle of wood studded with nails, and from every nail there hung a haddock. Its head had been cut off, and it hung by the *lug*, or ear. By-and-bye it became of a yellow tinge, and this deepened in colour with the length of exposure to the smoke. If the fish were to be eaten at once, or sold in the neighbourhood, they were smoked for only a short time. If they were to be sent to more distant markets in the south, they were smoked for a longer time, and more thoroughly cured. Fresh-caught fish, very slightly salted and smoked only to a golden yellow, had the greatest delicacy of flavour.

The fisher-folk, both men and women, were by no means averse to a *dram,* or glass of whiskey, but they were not drunkards. They were too frugal and thrifty to waste their money by continual drinking. They knew that their boats and nets were at the mercy of the sea and might any day be lost, and that boats and nets must in any case wear out and have to be renewed before many years were over. I have known a fisher-family stinting themselves even of their ordinary food in a time of scarcity, although they had over a hundred pounds in the house stored up against a still more evil day. The answer of Maggie Mucklebacket, the fisherwoman, to the Laird of Monkbarns, in Sir Walter Scott's novel of *The Antiquary*, was a valid apology, as the Laird allowed, for the occasional indulgence of the fishers in a dram. Monkbarns had been saying that he hoped the distilleries would never work again in his time. "Ay, ay," said Maggie, "its easy for your honour, and the like o' you gentlefolks, to say sae, that hae stouth and routh, and fire and fending, and meat and claith, and sit dry and canny by the fireside—but an ye wanted fire, and meat, and dry claise, and were deeing o' cauld, and had a sair heart, whilk is warst ava', wi' just tippence in your pouch, wadna ye be glad to buy a dram wi't, to be eilding and claise, and a supper and heart's ease into the bargain, till the morn's morning."

The social and domestic relations of husbands and wives among the fisher-folk is graphically sketched in Maggie's rejoinder to Jenny Rintherout, the female domestic of the Antiquary. Jenny had said to Maggie: " I maun hae a man that can mainteen his wife." "Ou ay, hinny," cried Maggie, "thae's your landward and burrows-town notions. My certie! fisher-wives ken better—they keep the man, and keep the house, and keep the siller, too, lass."

" A wheen poor drudges ye are," answered the nymph of the land to the nymph of the sea. " As soon as the keel o' the coble touches the sand, deil a bit mair will the lazy fisher-loons work, but the wives maun kilt their coats, and wade into the surf to tak' the fish ashore. And then the man casts off the wat and puts on the dry, and sits down wi' his pipe and his gillstoup ahint the ingle, like ony auld houdie, and ne'er a turn will he do till the coble's afloat again! And the wife, she maun get the scull on her back, and awa wi' the fish to the next burrows-town, and scauld and ban wi' ilka wife that will scauld and ban wi' her till it's sauld—and that's the gait fisher-wives live, puir slaving bodies."

" Slaves? gae wa', lass!—Ca' the head o' the house slaves? Little ye ken about it, lass. Show me a word my Saunders daur speak, or a turn he daur do about the house, without it be just to tak his meat, and his drink, and his diversion, like ony o' the weans. He has mair sense than to ca' ony thing about the bigging his ain, frae the rooftree down to a cracket trencher on the bink. He kens weel eneuch wha feeds him, and cleeds him, and keeps a' tight, thack and rape, when his coble is jowing awa in the Firth, puir fallow. Na, na, lass—them that sell the goods guide the purse—them that guide the purse rule the house. Show me ane o' your bits o' farmer-bodies that wad let their wife drive their stock to the market, and ca' in the debts. Na, na."

" In the fishing villages on the Friths of Forth and Tay, as well as elsewhere in Scotland," says Sir Walter in his notes, "the government is gynecoeracy, as described in the text." There is one illustrative point, however, which Sir Walter has not noticed. Among the married fishers the wife does not go by the name of the husband, but the husband goes by the name of the wife. The surnames in some of those fishing-villages are few in number, some three or four or five at the most. The Christian names are almost equally limited by the number of those of their kindred who have already borne them. To ask for Manson the fisherman, would be to ask in vain. There were many Mansons and all were fishermen. To ask for John Manson would be almost equally futile. Johns abounded in the family of Manson. If you asked for Jeanie's Jockie, you found your man at once. John Manson was the lawful husband and property of Jane Leeson. If there existed more than one Jane Leeson, you might have to ask for Maggie's Jeanie's Jockie.

It was a custom among The Cove fisher-folk in my time that if a fisher-lad and a fisher-lass were going to be married, they should, in company with their more immediate relations, go in state and formally give notice of their purpose to the Laird (*Anglicè*, Squire). This was probably a relic or survival from the old feudal times. I remember that on one occasion an engaged couple went with their following to tell the Laird. When he playfully rebuked them for bringing him stale news, which I had given him a month before, their answer was : " Eh, ay, but then ye ken he's ane o' oorsells." This was, I thought, the greatest compliment I had ever received in my life, and it would not have been a greater compliment to me if I had been admitted into one of the most exclusive clubs of London. So exclusive were the fishers in their own society and in their pride of race, that the fisher-children would not even play with the country children.

5.

I dare say that all this has vanished. I am talking of nearly thirty years ago. Even then the process of disintegration of thought and feeling was going on apace in the neighbouring town of Aberdeen. There was a unity of atmosphere between my daily intercourse with the fisher-folk and my daily poring over the pages of St. Thomas. In both there was an underlying stable element.

The *Summa* of St. Thomas was, as a Scottish Episcopalian parson once remarked to me, "a grand book to *howk* in" (*Anglicè* to dig in, or to quarry from). I *howked* like a day labourer, and in due time produced as the result of my digging and quarrying the volume which I christened *A Digest of St. Thomas on the Sacraments*. Even this labour, however, along with my ministries to the fisher-folk, did not exhaust my leisure time, and I went frequently into Aberdeen, which lay at the distance of only a four miles' walk, to assist the Rev. Mr. Comper, who succeeded Dr. Lee at Mr. Cheyne's old Church of St. John's. Mr. Comper was an Englishman, and the English Ritualistic movement was fast superseding the old Scottish Episcopalianism which was doctrinally so much akin to the elder Tractarianism.

The Rev. Mr. Comper found the same opposition in his ritualistic career at the hands of the Bishop of Aberdeen as did the Rev. Frederick George Lee. On December 6th, 1865, the Bishop wrote to the incumbent of St. John's: " It has been represented to me that you are in the habit of wearing, in some of your services in St. John's, coloured scarfs or stoles other than black, copes and chasubles, or some of them. Such vestments I hold to be unauthorized by our Church ; and it will be my duty to admonish you against the use of them. When taking duty for you in St. John's, some time last year, I was startled at finding candles, which had not been lighted at the beginning of the service, lighted just before I commenced the Office for the administration of the Lord's Supper. I at once put them out (!), but though I thus publicly marked my disapprobation of such a practice, I am given to understand that you still continue it. . . . I have therefore to request that you will inform me, (1) Whether on last Sunday, being the first Sunday in Advent, or on any other day during the present year, you did, while engaged in the Offices of the Church in St. John's, Aberdeen, wear any vestments, such as these before mentioned, or any other than the surplice ? (2) Whether on that day, or any other day during the present year, you caused the candles on the communion-table in your church to be lighted at the commencement of service for the administration of the Lord's Supper ? "

To this Mr. Comper replied : " I beg to say that, since I have been incumbent of St. John's, I have always worn an albe and a chasuble at the early celebration of the Holy Communion, but never at the eleven o'clock service ; that I have regularly worn coloured stoles, and that I have never worn a cope or other vestment except those mentioned and the surplice ; and, secondly, that I have always caused the candles on the altar to be lighted at the celebration of the Holy Communion. I may explain that I found all these usages established in the church, when I was appointed to the incumbency at Easter, 1861."

Mr. Comper's avowal produces Bishop Suther's ultimatum

"Did I believe that any arguments or entreaties of mine would induce you to adopt a different line of conduct, they should not be wanting, but I see no room for any such expectation, or for doubting that you are determined to disregard my remonstrances, and force me to take judicial proceedings against you. This, with whatever pain to myself, my duty calls on me to do ; and I therefore admonish you that the practices described in your letter are contrary to the laws and usages of the Church, and that, unless I receive from you, within five days, a written assurance that they will be hereafter discontinued, I must proceed against you in terms of the Canons."

I fancy that his lordship must have been consulting some one of my legal brethren in Aberdeen. The rest of his letter reads as if it had been written under advice. "To obviate any risk of misunderstanding, I annex the form of such an undertaking as I require : ' In compliance with the admonitions of my Bishop, I promise that I will not at any of the services in St. John's Church wear, or permit to be worn by the officiating clergyman, stoles or scarfs of any other colour than black, copes, chasubles, albs, or any other vestments than the usual surplice ; and that I will not allow the candles on the altar to be lighted at the commencement of the Communion Service, or to be used otherwise than for the necessary or actual purpose of affording light to the clergyman and choir.' "

By this *brutum fulmen* Mr. Comper is driven into a corner, and he acts on the principle that "half a loaf is better than no bread." He meets his ecclesiastical superior, the Ordinary of the diocese in which he is a subject, with this concession : "In compliance with your order, I will lay aside the use of coloured stoles, albe, and chasuble in the services of St. John's, so long as no authoritative interpretation different from that of your lordship is given of the Scottish Canon XXXII. concerning clerical vestments, or until you withdraw your order. . . . The question of lights on the altar during the celebration of Holy Communion rests, I conceive, on very different grounds. (1) I know of no law or Canon of the Scottish Church which in any way forbids them. (2) The practice is an established usage in St. John's of nearly fifteen years' standing. Lights have been used in the present new church ever since the consecration, at the early celebrations, and at all celebrations, so far as I can learn, for about fourteen years—a period extending through the whole of your lordship's episcopate, and a part of that of your venerated predecessor, and the incumbency of three successive pastors of St. John's. It has never to my knowledge been objected to, or remonstrated against by your predecessor or by your lordship ; for I may be allowed to say that I could not really regard the fact of your lordship having put out the candles, when officiating at St. John's eighteen months ago, when I was absent from home, as a remonstrance. (!) . . . I do not feel myself at liberty to accept your lordship's order in this matter as belonging to the class of admonitions which I promised at my ordination to obey. . . . It is from no spirit of disobedience, but from a deep sense of duty to the interests entrusted to my keeping as incumbent of a church where the usage has so long obtained that I feel myself under the necessity of declining to discontinue it, unless it shall be shown to be illegal or wrong."

What a revelation is not this of the real Presbyterianism of Scottish Episcopalianism !

I found myself at this time in Aberdeen at the "meeting of the waters." I was a link between the old school or system and the new. Like the older Tractarians, I cared more for the dogma and doctrine which the Tractarians had made their platform, while at the same time I regarded the new Ritualistic school as giving expression to the doctrinal teaching of the old-fashioned men. Of the confluence of the two streams—Scottish Episcopalian or Tractarian on the one hand, and modern Ritualistic on the other—I remember an amusing instance. A country clergyman had come to supply the place and take the duty of the ordinary pastor in one of the Ritualistic churches in Aberdeen. He had heard of chasubles and other "Eucharistic vestments," as they were called, and he was said to "sympathize with the vestments," but he had never seen them. When he arrived in the sacristy before eight o'clock, he found the vestments all laid out on the dressing-table, as in a Catholic sacristy. On the top there lay the amice. He took it up, and gazed at it. What to do with it was beyond him. Manfully following the light of nature, in the absence of either acquired information or infused knowledge, he proceeded to bind it, like a mason's apron, round his loins ! The attendant server was a sagacious boy. He was not so rude as to say, "That is not the way to put it on, sir." He said simply, "That is not the way, sir, we wear it *in this church.*" Instructed by the boy, my friend was following the instructions of the Roman ritual. His getting into the other vestments did not present the same difficulty, and he went forth to perform the Communion Service of the Church of England, firmly persuaded that in so doing he was saying Mass, and in those vestments fancying himself every inch a priest.

6.

In the neighbouring town of Aberdeen, my native town, I found among the High Churchmen, both clerical and lay, congenial society. At The Cove I had only the Laird, and I think that I preferred to him the society of the fishers, and most certainly the society of St. Thomas. In Aberdeen, at this period of my history, all had changed or was fast changing. It was a period of transition, a time of disintegration both in the educational and in the religious spheres. Marischal College—the "Mareschall College of Aberdeen," of which Dugald Dalgetty of Drumthwacket was always talking, in season and out of season, at every period of his adventures— was no longer in itself a University. It had been amalgamated with King's College in the one University of Aberdeen, with new ways to which I was a stranger, although at the time of the amalgamation I qualified and was established for life as a member of the General Council of the united University.

My old school, too, had disappeared—that is to say, the old school-buildings, and along with them the old school system. Latin we were well taught in my old school. It was the only thing that we really learned, and it was literally whipped into us. Beginning with Ruddiman's *Rudiments* and the *Colloquies* of Corderius, we read Cornelius Nepos, Cæsar, Virgil, Horace, Ovid, Cicero, and Livy. Every Saturday we had a *version.* A piece of English was dictated to us by the master, and this we had then and there to turn into Latin, with the aid of a volume called the *Grammatical Exercises* and Ainsworth's *Dictionary,* which was the dictionary in almost universal use in the school. These books, along with pens, ink, and paper, we brought with us on the version-days. Our translations, or *versions,* we handed to the master as soon as they were finished, and the rest of the time was at our own disposal in the class-room. On the following Wednesday afternoon the versions were brought back, marked with the number of errors, or with an O, as *sine errore.* The errors were divided into three classes— *maximus, medius,* and *minimus* errors. Then began the practical business of the afternoon. *Medius* and *minimus* errors went unpunished, although they counted in the allotting of our places on the benches or *factions,* as they were called. Our names, along with the number of errors for which we were individually responsible, were read out, and we changed our places on the factions, up or down as the case might be. These benches were arranged like the pews in a church, on both sides of the class-room, leaving a passage in the middle, and all facing the master's desk, a rostrum which was raised three steps above the level of the floor. The factions held five boys apiece. The book-boards of them were carved all over with names, which gave testimony to the industry of our predecessors for generations with their pocketknives. Among these names was that of Lord Byron, who was at this school before he succeeded to the title and went to Harrow. His mother was a Miss Gordon of Gight, and during his childhood he and she lived in Aberdeen. When all the boys were seated in due order, the master began his correction of the writers in strict accordance with his previous correction of their versions. The first boy who had made a *maximus* error, on hearing his name read out as coupled with that fact, left his place and went to the master's desk, stood in front of it, and held out his hand, and received on his open palm one " pandy," if he had made one *maximus* error only. If he had made two, he received two pandies, or twenty pandies if he had made twenty errors, and so in like proportion in accordance with the strict rule of distributive justice. The pandies took their name from *Pande manum*—" Stretch out your open hand " —and were administered by the master with the *tawse,* from the top step of his desk on which he stood. The *tawse* was a broad leather strap, one end of which was divided into five fingers about six inches long, and these had been scorched in the fire to harden them and make them more stinging. On receiving his allowance, which was given and taken with the utmost calm on both sides, the boy returned to his place and resumed his conversation with his next neighbour. Conversation was general while the whipping went on, and as there were seventy boys in my class, the rest of the afternoon was usually occupied in this way. Other afternoons which were spent in a similar manner were those on which we had repetitions. Thirty lines of Ovid or of Virgil were usually given out the day before to be learned by heart, and of these any boy might be called on promiscuously to repeat five lines. Most of us generally learned five lines only, on the off-chance of our getting those five lines. If these did not fall to our lot, there were always boys in front of us, behind us, or on either side of us, with their books open before them, who prompted us, so that we were very often able to stagger through. If all means failed, we went to the master's desk and got our pandies, which for this shortcoming did not as a rule exceed five in number. On other days the whipping was less general, although there were few days which were entirely unmarked by it in some one's remembrance. No one resented his punishment, or was made unhappy by it, and I never heard of its doing any one any harm.

The most extraordinary case of whipping that I remember occurred on occasion of a complaint made by the police about our having broken the windows of an unpopular neighbour. The question was put by the master, the catalogue was called, and every boy had to answer to his name either Yes or No. Every boy answered No. The master jumped up in great excitement, and shouted, "Gentlemen, there is a liar in the school, but I'll get at him," and he proceeded forthwith to whip the whole class of seventy boys, from the *Dux* at the top, to the dunce at the bottom of the class. His method of getting at the liar was not so entirely without reason as it might at first sight appear to be. Lying in order to escape punishment was almost the only sin which was recognized by our school code of morality. Our master knew that the delinquent must be known to some of us. He knew also that no one of us would peach upon him, but he knew, moreover, that that boy would have an evil time at the hands of every one of us when we got at him out of school. His ingenious wisdom was justified by the event.

Our master's name was John Dun. This surname was famous in the school. It was the name of one who, if not its founder some centuries before, had been at least its greatest benefactor. In the appointment of masters, preference was given to one of the name of Dun, if he was otherwise fairly well qualified for the post. Our John Dun was a good Latin scholar, and his faithfulness in the discharge of his duty of whipping Latin into us was without a flaw. Outside the school he was a most good-natured

and kind-hearted man, and the best whipped boys were as
eager as any for the honour of walking home with him to his
lodging in an old turreted house, which was entered from one
of the courts or closes on the School Hill.

The school house was a quaint old building, the ground-plan
of which was laid on the lines of a capital H.   It contained four
class-rooms, and a large room which ran along the whole length
of the building, and was called the Public School.   Its place
would be represented by the central bar of the letter H.   The
four portions of the letter above and below this bar, give the
situation of the four class-rooms, all of which opened into the
Public School.   The Public School was used only on public
occasions, such as the annual examination and giving of prizes,
which was held in state by the Provost and Baillies (*Anglicè*,
Mayor and Aldermen) of Aberdeen, and the Professors of
Marischal College and University.   It was used also for the
dictation of the trial *version*, at the annual competition for the
bursaries in connection with Marischal College.   These bursaries
were many in number, although small in value, ranging from
five pounds to twenty pounds.   This money was the annual
interest of various foundations, or *mortifications*, as they were
called in the law language of Aberdeen.   Some of the
bursaries were of considerable antiquity, and many of them
were privileged in favour of certain surnames, or of the natives
of certain parishes or counties.   The holding of a bursary carried
also with it abatements in College fees.   Small as was their
money value, the bursaries served their purpose in making it
possible for the sons of poor persons to secure a good classical
education, and through this an entrance to the learned professions of divinity, law, and medicine.   Many Scotchmen of
eminence have attained to it by means of those bursaries, and
of the school which qualified them for the gaining of the
bursaries.   To get, however, to the foundation and root of the
successful careers of those men, we must go to the parish schools
of Scotland, as they were in my time. Every country parish had
its parochial school, which was frequented by the children of
farm servants and of the smaller farmers.   The masters of those
schools were, for the most part, young Presbyterian ministers
or divinity students who were waiting for a church, and were in
the meantime called probationers and could take occasional
Sunday duty.   Some were content to remain schoolmasters all
their lives, and they were in fact better off than were many of

the parish ministers. They had almost as much money by way of income as had the ministers, and there were not so many calls upon their purses. They gave an excellent education to their pupils in the three R's, and in the elements of history and geography. Nearly all of them had a Latin class, which any of the scholars could attend for a very small additional payment. With the best of their scholars, the *Dominies*, as the school-masters were commonly called, very often took great pains, and not seldom such pains as to fit them for joining the Rector's classes—the fourth and fifth—at the Public School in Aberdeen, without having passed through the three junior classes, as we did. The fourth and fifth classes were held in one class-room, and were taught by the Rector. We now began to learn Greek, and mathematics in the shape of Euclid. Hitherto we had learned nothing but Latin, except during one hour a week, when we were taught history, and one other hour, when we were taught geography. The teaching of these subjects had been an innovation. They were not taught in my father's time, when the whole of the education given was purely classical. Arithmetic was not taught, even in my time, in the Public School of Aberdeen. For that we had to go, at twelve o'clock, to one or other of two private schools of writing and arithmetic in the town.

In the Rector's school-room there were no *pandies*. It must not, however, be supposed that the relief from the possibility of pandies was reckoned as a privilege. To be summoned, after dismissal of the class, into the awful presence of the Rector, was in our eyes more dreadful than any number of pandies ever was, or could possibly have been. Standing for judgment before his desk, we quaked with terror. The Rector was an absolute monarch within his school dominions, and capital punishment, in the shape of expulsion, was the only sentence uttered at his tribunal. An appeal, indeed, was possible to the municipal authorities—the Lord Provost and the Baillies—but in the tradition of the school was imbedded the solid fact that no such appeal had ever in the memory of man been once sustained. The Provost and the Baillies were always on the side of authority, as vested in the Rector of the school, whatever they might, in their private capacities, have thought of his action as being either right or wrong. The only case of expulsion in my time, was that of a boy for stealing books. For this poor wretch there was no sympathy. He had disgraced us all, and all felt relieved in being rid of the pollution of his presence. Stealing was, in our eyes, an even greater sin than that of lying in order to escape the punishment of *pandies.* Open and forcible robbery of books would not have excited the same horror and disgust. *Væ victis* would have been the verdict of the majority of those boys who had not been made the victims of the robbery, and this might have been rendered in the vernacular as, "the weakest must go to the wall," or metrically, as the outcome of—

> The good old rule, the simple plan,
> That he should take who has the power
> And he should keep who can.

If the theft had been committed by the father of the boy in his own school-days, the punishment would not have been mere expulsion. Previous to his expulsion he would have been *portered.* There was no instance of *portering* in my time. It had not been abolished, however, and a case of it would not have been regarded as an arbitrary introduction of a punishment which was not indigenous in the system of the school. To all of us the details of it were familiar from tradition. A case of it certainly occurred during my father's school-days. It was carried out in this way. All the boys in the five classes were solemnly assembled in the Public School. The catalogue was called, and every boy who was present answered to his name *Adsum,* as he had to answer every morning when the catalogue of his class was called in his own class-room. The culprit was then stripped, and mounted entirely naked on the back of the school porter, who marched from end to end of the long room, followed by the Rector, who went on flogging the boy continuously throughout his progress. His clothes were then returned to him, and he was led to the main door, which was opened. From the top of the three or four stone steps which led down into the paved courtyard, he received a kick from the Rector, and the ceremony was complete. A curious incident is connected with the last instance of *portering* of which I have heard. While the boy was being disrobed for the function, he took his knife from his pocket and stabbed himself in the breast. The Rector carefully and kindly examined the wound, and found it to be but trifling. He saw, moreover, that the motive was more histrionic than tragic, and the ceremony proceeded with every solemnity, till it was crowned by the final kick.

The school-boy of to-day, who is petted and overfed at home, and who knows a very little of everything under the sun, may shudder at what seem to him to be the barbarities of those days, as he may sneer at the smallness of the information with which in those days boys left school. We certainly were turned out as ignorant as owls of all the *ologies* and *isms* and other miscellaneous information with which the modern boy is crammed at school—but we were turned out *educated*, so far as our education went. In spite of our little studying, or studying as little as we could help, a knowledge of the Latin tongue had somehow soaked its way into us, and this with even scholarship and elegance of composition. In Greek we never arrived at scholarship. We began the study of Greek too late in our school career, and although the Rector had a very fair knowledge of the Greek language, he was not in any way in Greek as he was in Latin, a master of style. We were taught only so much as was required for matriculation at Marischal College and University, and that was only the Gospel of St. John and Xenophon's *Anabasis*. At the College we read Homer and Anacreon, Herodotus and Thucydides, but we never got such a grip of these as we had got of the Latin authors. Dr. Brown, the Greek Professor, had a somewhat broad Scotch accent, and from it he was dubbed The Dorian. He was never spoken of among us by any other name. He was powerless to keep order, in spite of his continual expostulations. In the class-room of Dr. Cruikshank, the Professor of Mathematics, the order was perfect. Sir Walter Scott's quack had just "twa simples" for every disease, namely, "laudamy and calamy" (laudanum and calomel) — "simples with a vengeance," said Sir Walter. Old Cruikie had one simple only for the disease of disorder, and that was—expulsion. It might have been said of him what the Duke of Wellington said of General Picton, when an official of the commissariat complained to him that Picton had said he would hang him if a certain number of cattle were not forthcoming on a particular day for the consumption of the army. "Did Picton say that?" asked Wellington. "I know Picton. He's a man of his word. I should advise you to get up those cattle." We all knew that Dr. Cruikshank was equally a man of his word, and for anything like insubordination he would have decimated his class for the common good. He was withal a kind-hearted man, and we knew him to be inflexibly just. Hence it was that he secured from every one that respect apart from which a general *timor reverentialis* is impossible. This The Dorian never could command, and scholarship in Greek suffered in consequence. I can certainly corroborate from my own experience a statement which has been made, I forget where, in print, that Scotland has never produced a Greek scholar. Some Scotsmen have been Grecians, but they had their training, not in Scotland, but in the Public Schools and Universities of England. This may perhaps no longer be the case. I am speaking of my own time.

In my time I "stood in the midst of the years." The old systems were passing away during my residence at The Cove, and were giving place to new systems in the spheres both of education and of religion. Railways had been for some time bringing Scotland into closer communication with England, and English ideas and methods in both spheres were creeping towards the north. With the full flowing of this tide the old-fashioned systems of stern discipline and solid education were being fast obliterated. Scottish Episcopalianism, with its stiff doctrinalism, and with its absence of even decent ritual, was being swept away into the remoter districts by a wave of Anglicanism which was less Tractarian than it was Ritualistic.

This was what I found on my frequent visits to Aberdeen from my solitude at The Cove. I returned from them to The Cove as to a haven of rest, with its bracing salt-sea breezes, its simple ways, and the stick-in-the-mud conservatism of the fisher-folk. Little did the fishers care about the changes that were taking place outside their community in the educational and religious world. They were not aware even of the existence of those changes. Few of them could either read or write, but they could catch fish, cure fish, carry fish to market, and in a bargain for the sale of fish could beat those who had more school learning than they had. They were wise in their generation. They were educated for their state of life.

7.

Life at The Cove with these surroundings, and with St. Thomas to feed, and fatten, and fructify one's soul, was an ideal and an idyllic life, if one could only have been *absolutely* sure that we were one with St. Thomas, not merely in understanding and in will, or in soul only, but also as members of one body—that external society of Christians which

D

constitutes Christ's visible Church. We thought that we were, and we honestly thought that we were. We not only regretted, but we abhorred, the revolution in religion which we could scarcely bring ourselves to call the Reformation. Our platform was this. Three centuries ago there had been a quarrel between England and Rome. Like most family quarrels, there were faults on both sides. We were heirs of evil consequences, but certainly not authors of the cause of them. We could not therefore be schismatics. Even if it should turn out that our forefathers had been formally schismatical in their separation of themselves from the rest of Christendom, their sin could not possibly lie at our doors, who were daily praying for the Reunion of Christendom. Neither again were we borrowing our spiritual food from any foreign source. We were being taught by a Doctor of the Universal Church. St. Thomas had happened in God's providence to belong to the Latin branch of the Church Catholic, and some of his opinions might reflect his surroundings, but, given all this, he was no small authority, if not the greatest authority, in doctrinal matters, in that Church of which we fondly fancied that both he and we were fellow-members. We did not therefore feel that in appropriating the doctrine of St. Thomas we were either borrowing or stealing. That which rendered this view possible to us was the fact that the highest conception which we had of the Universal Church was that of a congeries or confederation of particular Churches, or dioceses, of the aggregate of which the Bishop of Rome was head by ecclesiastical right, derived from concession or consent of the whole Church. We regarded the Roman Pontificate as a natural evolution, or as a consequence in reason, but we had not grasped the idea of its existence as of *Divine* right, and resting on the institution and constitution of Jesus Christ.

My life at The Cove for three years, with the fishers and St. Thomas, was brought to an end by my presentation to the living of St. Mary Magdalene's, Dundee. It was in the gift of the Bishop of Brechin, whom I had consulted about my Roman difficulties, and who had given me Anglican Orders. He had his Cathedral in Dundee, although he took his title from the town of Brechin. Brechin had been one of the ancient Catholic sees, but was now a mere market-town. Dundee was a great centre of commercial industry. It had been enriched both by the jute-trade and by whaling enterprise. The population consisted of about one hundred thousand inhabitants, of whom one-fourth, or about five-and-twenty thousand, were Roman Catholics of Irish extraction, and in the second or third generation from the date of their immigration. My appointment to Dundee would have been regarded by most of my fellow-parsons as promotion. To me it was transportation from a most congenial atmosphere to a most uncongenial sphere. It was a wrench to leave The Cove.

The Bishop was a timid man and—mindful of my Roman leanings, which I had from the outset of my connection with his diocese laid bare before him—used every effort to make me consent to a condition which he proposed in connection with his presentation of me to this living. The condition was that if ever I should decide to become a Roman Catholic, I should not make my submission to the Roman Catholic Church within six months after my resignation of the living of St. Mary Magdalene's. To this condition I objected, but ultimately agreed to refer the question to my confessor, Canon Humble, of St. Ninian's Cathedral, Perth. Canon Humble was in this matter equal to the occasion. He told me that on no account should I agree to this condition—that it was morally false and wrong. He said that the very first Roman priest whom I consulted would tell me that I was in no way bound by my promise or contract—that it was *pactum illicitum*—that I had been weak to make it, and that I should be wicked to keep it, since, in the case supposed, I should be formally in bad faith, and living, therefore, during those six months, in the state of damnation. His advice was most sound. I retailed it to my Bishop, and ultimately, without any condition whatsoever, he instituted me to my living. I now found myself in the midst of very different surroundings, and in a very different atmosphere from that of The Cove.

My congregation at Dundee was mainly composed of Orange Irishmen. There were very few Scottish Episcopalians among them. The bulk of my people had come from Ulster, or the north of Ireland, and in their own land they had belonged to what was humorously called—in the days before Mr. Gladstone and his Disestablishment—the UNITED Church of England and Ireland. My predecessor was a scholar and an author, a man

who used to write for *The Christian Remembrancer*, a publication which held then very much the same place as does *The
Church Quarterly* of to-day, or *The British Critic* of former
times. He was a student and a smoker, and the Bishop used
to say that his "study stank of metaphysics and tobacco."
He had not, however, neglected his congregation, and he had
indoctrinated the younger portion of his people with High
Church ideas. I found, therefore, two schools and camps of
religious thought and practice within my one congregation.
The older people were sternly Protestant—their children were
strongly inclined towards a High Churchism which was a
contradiction and condemnation of the religion of their elders.

Even with the elders, however, I was personally popular.
Their only objection to me was, that I never preached against
the idolatrous principles and practices of Rome. Their
doctrinal attitude may be gauged by the following incident.
Our altar was vested in variously coloured frontals, in accordance
with the ecclesiastical seasons. On one Sunday it happened to
be vested in *green*. This Sunday turned out to have been
the anniversary of the Battle of the Boyne. Of this battle I
may have heard the name, but in it I had absolutely no interest
whatever. My older people had, and they supposed that on
this particular day I had hoisted the Roman Catholic colours
to show my sympathy with the Roman Catholic religion.

That, however, which brought matters to a crisis was the
feast of the Immaculate Conception. I told the people to turn
to their prayer-books, and there they would find set down for
celebration the feast of the *Conception B.V.M.* I argued that
a maculate or stained conception could not possibly be com-
memorated by any feast, and therefore that, by direction of the
Church of England, we ought to celebrate the Immaculate, or
stainless, Conception of our Lady, and that in so doing we
ought to congratulate ourselves that in this at any rate we
were not at issue with our brethren of the great Latin Church
throughout the world. We kept the feast with splendour. The
altar was radiant with lights and lilies. The devotion of the
younger part of the congregation was immense. The dismay
and the disgust of their fathers and mothers were intense.
The senior churchwarden interviewed me. He said sorrow-
fully—for personally he liked me—and in the best of good
faith, that he must present me for false doctrine to the
Bishop. I cordially agreed with him from his point of view,

and begged him to do so at once This somewhat sobered him. Even so, he went like a man to do his duty. His will was better than his judgment. The long list of the articles of his impeachment of me contained the most cherished articles of the Bishop's own belief. The only difference between us was that Dr. Forbes in preaching wrapped up his High Church doctrine in Low Church language, while I delivered the self-same doctrine in words the meaning of which no man could possibly mistake. The Bishop was in a quandary. If he condemned me, he would be condemning himself, and he knew that I was teaching that which he himself had taught me. It was contained in his own writings. His answer to the Irish Orangeman was characteristic of the man, who on his trial for false doctrine had pleaded that opinions, which he believed to be revealed truths, with regard to the Eucharist, were permissible within the pale of the Church of England, and were at any rate not such as to entail upon him penal consequences for his promulgation of them. He said to my accuser : " Have you got five hundred pounds to spend ? If I were to condemn and suspend your pastor, he might bring me before the Court of Session (the highest civil tribunal in Scotland) for defamation of character and unwarranted and wanton destruction of his clerical career. Are you prepared to lodge five hundred pounds in bank ? Until you do I cannot undertake to judge the case." The old man went away sorrowful, since he had not this amount of spare riches at his disposal.

I used to see a great deal of the Bishop during my residence in Dundee. He was a fascinating man, with most charming manners. His conversation was refined, instructive, and somewhat cynical. I met Dean Ramsay at his house, who came to pay a visit at the same time that I was staying with the Bishop for some weeks before I entered on possession of my living. The Dean—he was Dean of Edinburgh—was a thorough old-fashioned Scottish Episcopalian. In his church there was little that the modern Ritualist would recognize as Ritualism, but all things were, as the Dean would have put it, done " decently and in order." In doctrine he was somewhat nebulous outside the sphere of belief in Baptismal Regeneration, the three-fold ministry, the propriety of Confirmation, and some vague presence of Christ in the Eucharist, a presence which had much better not be too clearly and closely defined.

Dean Ramsay's book of *Reminiscences of Scottish Wit and Humour*, is as familiar to most fairly-educated Scotchmen as are household words, and it is by no means unknown on the wrong side of the Tweed. His stories in conversation were equally racy. He was one of the last of Edinburgh men who could speak the old Court Scotch, which differed considerably from "broad Scotch" as spoken by the lower orders. He had a coterie of old ladies, his contemporaries, who used to take a "dish of tea" with him at stated and frequent intervals, and converse in the old Court dialect. All this has passed away. The Dean enjoyed his visit to the Bishop immensely, and after his departure wrote to thank him for the pleasure it had given him. The Bishop read us his letter. Thanking his host for his hospitality, and expressing his satisfaction with all the arrangements for his comfort, the Dean wound up by saying that he had been much edified by what the Bishop had said to him about the theological erudition of his curates, and their proficiency in the study of St. Thomas ; but there was one thing he must venture to remark, and that was that never in all his life had he seen a grouse so foully murdered as by one of them. This censure I took home to myself. I had sat beside the Dean at breakfast, and before me were some cold grouse. One of these was a tough old cock, and in the dissection of him I had nearly as much bodily fatigue as I had mental disturbance from observing that my labours were being attentively watched by the Dean. The Bishop's comment on the Dean's remark was as consoling as it was cynical. He said : " I fancy that good Mr. Dean values carving more than he does theology as a clerical accomplishment."

I have spoken of Canon Humble, of Perth. He was my confessor. The Canon was also Precentor of St. Ninian's Cathedral in that city. St. Ninian's was, like Cumbrae, an exotic. It has also, and like Cumbrae, been described as an ecclesiastical hothouse. Like Cumbrae, moreover, it was supposed to be not an Anglican plant, but a flower of very Scottish Episcopalian growth. It was officered, however, chiefly by Englishmen of an advanced type. In my time only two of these remained. One was the Precentor, Canon Humble. The other was the Provost, Mr. Edward Knottesford Fortescue, who some years later, and after his second marriage, became a Catholic. They were my nearest congenial clerical neighbours, and we three were fast friends. In the earlier days of St. Ninian's the ritual had been very insignificant, if measured by the standard of the principles and practice of modern Ritualists. It was always, however, developing. When, at each fresh step in the process of evolution, the old-fashioned Scotch Episcopalians would ask the meaning of the new rite, the answer was always, "ancient Scottish use." They might have disrelished if not resisted an Anglican importation, but any rite, however unfamiliar, which was presented to them as a genuine product of Scottish soil, appealed at once to both their national and their antiquarian instincts.

Both the Provost and the Precentor of St. Ninian's Cathedral were at loggerheads with the Bishop of the diocese. This was Dr. Charles Wordsworth. He had been the first Warden of Glenalmond College, and by means of his own vote, which gave him a majority of votes in the electing chapter, he had made his way from Glenalmond into the Protestant bishopric of St. Andrew's, Dunkeld and Dunblane. St. Ninian's was his Cathedral, but for many years he had never entered it, and he refused to enter it so long as doctrines were preached and rites were practised of which he could not approve. There stood in the chancel a Gothic episcopal throne. It struck the Provost that as this was never occupied by the Bishop, it might reasonably be utilized by the clergy. He had therefore a piece of perforated zinc let into the side of it by way of grille, and then sat in it and heard confessions. I have myself knelt at that throne and made my confession.

I felt more at home with the clergy at St. Ninian's than I did with my own Bishop Forbes at Dundee. We two, nevertheless, the Bishop and I, had much in common, and there were some functions in which we were confederates. These were the consecration of holy oils and the consecration of altar-stones. I used to go to the marble-cutters and to the chemists, and procured the stones duly incised with five crosses, and the oil and balsam wherewith to make the chrism, and then the Bishop did his best with a Roman Pontifical. Dundee was at that time regarded as an emporium of these sacred luxuries, by the more advanced members of the Puseyite party. Like Dr. Pusey himself, his disciple Dr. Forbes had not the most rudimentary conception of ecclesiastical jurisdiction. Their one idea of all that was necessary for the doing of episcopal or sacerdotal acts was possession of power of order, episcopal or sacerdotal, as the case might be. Just as Dr. Pusey was in the habit of making confession tours throughout the length and breadth of England, and giving absolution without receiving any faculties to do so from the Protestant Bishops within whose dioceses he was sojourning, so was Bishop Forbes in the habit of exporting his holy oils and altar-stones into the dioceses of Bishops who would have regarded them as contraband. I remember an amusing instance of the then all but universal ignorance or ignoring of the first principles of jurisdiction. An Anglican Bishop highly disapproved both of the doctrines and of the practices of one of the dignitaries of his diocese. To deprive a Rector of his living was, however, an expensive process, and from this the Bishop shrank. There was not the same difficulty in withdrawing the licences of his curates, and this the Bishop did. On the following Sunday the Rector told his people what the Bishop had done, and said that his curates would now no longer be able to say Matins and Evensong, or to celebrate the Communion Service, but that they could still read the Lessons, and visit the sick, and hear confessions, that being a matter with which the Bishop had nothing whatever to do!

8.

About this time one of my oldest friends was received into the Catholic Church. I had often thought that if ever this parson should "go over to Rome," I should be sorely shaken in my allegiance to the Church of England. When I heard that he had actually been received, I was surprised to find how little the news affected me. By-and-bye my friend wrote to me and told me what he had done, and expressed his earnest hope that his action would not interfere with our old friendship, as it had done in the case of so many of his friends. I wrote to assure him that on the continuance of our friendship he might depend, that I knew for certain that he had taken the step in simple obedience to the dictates of his conscience, and that I myself would gladly follow him, if only I could see my way. I added that, although I was determined to let no earthly consideration stand in the way if I should ever see it to be my duty, I as matter of fact had never felt less inclined to leave the Church of England for the Church of Rome than I did at that moment. My friend's answer contained simply his thanks for the pleasure my letter had given him in its assurance about the continuance of our old friendship. On controversy, he said, he would not enter, as I knew the points at issue as well as he did, but that he had a strong feeling that erelong I should find my way into the Catholic and Roman Church, or that I would not at any rate die outside it.

There was nothing to disturb me in his letter which I read during breakfast on a Monday morning, on my return from what I then supposed to be my Mass, which I was in the habit of saying daily at eight o'clock. I went into my study and sat down to St. Thomas, whose *Summa* lay always open on my table. There lay there also the proofs of the last sheets of my Digest of his doctrine on the Incarnation, which was then passing through the press and was almost ready for publication. I began, however, to feel restless, and I could not concentrate my attention on the correction of the proofs. My friend's words about finding my way into the Roman Catholic Church before I died, to which I had given but little heed while reading them, kept coming before my mind and distracting me. That it was *possible* that I might some day become a Roman Catholic was certain. That it was not *probable* I was by no means sure. Then came the question, vividly presenting itself, and seeming as it were imperatively to demand an instant answer: "Supposing you were to die to-day, and to-day to stand for judgment before your Maker, what are the solid reasons, such as would hold water, that you could give for not having died a Roman Catholic?" I could not give to myself any reasons that satisfied me, and nevertheless at the same time it did not seem to me that I had reasons which would justify me in leaving the sphere in which I found myself in the providence of God. One thing alone was clear to me, and that was that something must be done by me, and at once. I must take action this very day to bring the matter to an issue, and come to a decision. The result of my self-communing was that I determined to go at once to London, and see my friend, and hear all and everything that he had to say. If his reasons convinced me, I should straightway follow his example. If, on the other hand, his reasons failed to convince me, I should return to my work with my mind at rest, and free from any doubt to disturb its peace. To leave my post was not so easy. I was working at St. Mary's single-handed, with my daily Mass and evening service—three services every Sunday, and sometimes four—two catechism classes every week, a couple of 'week-day Lenten sermons, for Lent had begun—some sick-visiting, and about forty confessions a week to hear. I made arrangements, however, to leave Dundee for three days, and with hope within my heart that I should be back home again on the third day, a happy and reinvigorated man, disburdened from every doubt, and no one having had any knowledge of what had happened. There was a pledge of this hope in my leaving St. Thomas lying open as usual upon my study-table. That there was along with this hope in my mind some dread that I might be leaving my home for ever, is pointed to by the provision which I made for this event in drawing out whatever money I had at my bankers, and in taking with me an amount of luggage for an absence of three days, which I learned in after-years had caused my old housekeeper, who knew my habits, no small surprise.

I left Dundee for London by the night mail-train, and my meditations were unbroken by any sleep. The Church of England came before my mind as moribund, rent with schism, and riddled with heresy, and with scarcely any right to rank among the living branches of the Church of Christ. For a long time I had most painfully felt the absence in her of the *bene esse,* but this absence had seemed to me to be still compatible with the existence of the *esse* of a Church or component part of that congeries of particular Churches which had hitherto constituted in my mind the Universal Church.

When the night was at its darkest the day began to dawn. Slowly from out the chaos in my mind of contending Churches —Roman, Greek, and Anglican, and parties in conflict within the latter—there rose up the Divine idea in all its beauty of the one and only Church of Christ—the one Body with the one Spirit—as not only one and undivided, as in the ages before the division between East and West, but as one and *indivisible*. This I now knew that it ever was, and ever would be, if for no other reason than because it ever *must* be. The delusion of the branch theory, to which I had clung so long, was laid bare before me in the nakedness of its absurdity. The supreme moment—which is the first moment after the last moment of unbelief—had come—the grace of God had been vouchsafed to me—and with actual faith I at last believed in the One, Catholic, Apostolic, and Roman Church of God, as the one visible and indivisible Church of Christ upon the earth.

The struggle in my mind was over before the train reached London, and I had no longer either desire or need to listen to anything that my friend might have to say. I was as convinced as he was, and all that he could do for me would be to arrange for my submission, and that without delay. One comic difficulty occurred to me as I was nearing London. I was dressed like a Roman Catholic priest, and now I felt like an impostor in a Roman collar. I solved the difficulty by removing the linen band, and retaining the black stock. In this guise I arrived at my friend's lodging, but only to find that he had left town for some days. The servant, however, informed me that the other reverend gentleman who was staying with my friend was at home. This was another clerical convert whom I knew by name, and who also in the same way knew me. I sent in my card, and was received most courteously and, when I made known to him my errand, most cordially. All I wanted was a sheet of paper to write my resignation of my living. This done, he overwhelmed me with hospitality, but I could not eat. In my friend's absence he volunteered to take me to Archbishop Manning, who lived close by in York Place. To that I was somewhat averse, but only for this reason that we Puseyites somehow did not take to Dr. Manning in the same way as we were inclined to take to Dr. Newman, although Dr. Newman had said the hardest things about the Anglican position, and things which Dr. Manning had refrained from saying or had softened down. I said to my new found friend that I would wait an hour or two and talk over with him the priests in London to whom I might go to be received. He advised me, instead of talking, to go and lie down upon his bed and try to get some sleep, and he would manage the whole affair for me. I did his bidding, and slept profoundly for three or four hours, and on rejoining him I was rather taken aback to hear that in the interval he had been to Dr. Manning, had told him my story, and had arranged that I should hear his Grace's Mass next morning at eight o'clock, thereafter breakfast with him, and then have an interview. This was more than I had bargained for, but I thought to myself, " In for a pound, in for a penny." One Catholic priest will be very much the same as another, and after all it does not very much matter by whom I am received. This has happened apart from any voluntary action of mine, and there seems to me no solid reason why I should not swing with the tide in what may perchance be the providence of God.

I have ever since been most glad that I made my submission to the Catholic Church in the hands of Dr. Manning. No one could have been more kind than his Grace was to me. He insisted on my coming to his house, and spending some days with him. Father Herbert Vaughan (now Cardinal Vaughan) was staying there at the same time, and I remember it on account of a subsequent remark of his that when he first saw me I looked like a frontispiece to the Seven Penitential Psalms! I was then in my Roman collar from which the day before I had removed the linen band, as the easiest way out of the difficulty about my clerical dress, until I should have time to make other arrangements. Seeing Dr. Manning's eyes fixed upon my neck-gear, I told him my story, and that this was only a makeshift till I could provide myself with a tie, and other secular attire. "By no means," he said, "make no change in your dress, and resume your Roman collar, which I now give you right to wear, as a possible candidate for the priesthood."

"There is one question," said the Archbishop during my stay with him, "that I want to ask you, but only for a reason which regards a view of my own. You need not answer it unless you like, but for years past I have asked it, for my own information, of all the many parsons whom I have received. Do you consider that during all your clerical life you have been living in the ministry of the Church of England in good faith?" I answered without hesitation, "Undoubtedly I do, and it seems to me that I have proved it by the manner of my coming." "Precisely," he rejoined, "and just the answer I expected, and the only answer I have ever got to my question. I have heard of parsons who were said to be living in bad faith, but I have never yet met with one of them of whom I was certain that he was not in what seemed to him to be good faith, and I have never received a single parson who could admit that he had been consciously ministering in bad faith."

9.

I must here interrupt my narrative to record what took place in my church in Dundee after I had left it. This will be best described by some quotations from a pamphlet which was published at the time, and it was an open secret that it came from the pen of a Redemptorist Father, since deceased, but who was then living at the Redemptorist Convent on Kinnoul Hill, in the neighbourhood of Perth, and at no great distance from

Dundee. "The congregation of St. Mary Magdalene's," he writes, "is divided into two hostile camps, each making opposite demands on their chief pastor, and threatening, it would appear, in case no satisfactory arrangement can be made, to separate from one another altogether. . . . One side are averse to flowers and to lights on the altar, to choral services, and to certain vestments which have come into use. The other side desire what they call full choral services, petition for flowers, lights, and other decorations, for vestments of the proper colour, and pray that the altar be no more desecrated. Now, at first sight, or to those who have not looked beneath the surface, a religious war for such objects may perhaps appear ridiculous. What folly, they say, to contend so fiercely about vases of flowers, and wax candles, and silken vestments ; are Episcopalians going to sacrifice their boasted unity for such trifles ? Yet, after all, these contending parties are Dundee citizens, and Dundee citizens are not generally fools. They have raised their old burgh to the city of third importance in Scotland, and have shown themselves no children in their competition with the great ones of the world. . . . As reasonable, sensible persons they must find something beneath these exteriors really worth the contending for—something which men of principle and piety consider to be of great value. On the one hand, it may be fairly argued that no man of sense could reasonably object to things so innocent in themselves as flowers and lights and vestments being used in the worship of God, nor even, should such ornaments not coincide with his peculiar taste, could he ever dream of making them a cause of ferocious strife and disunion. . . . There must then be some strong reason which induces the petitioners to stand out so determinedly against the use of these things. On the other hand, why should the opposite side insist upon them ? They are fully aware that decoration and music are not necessary ; they know that from rocks and caves and dens of the earth adoration and prayer have ascended to God, at least as agreeable to Him as any they can offer with all their festal splendour. Why, then, contend so stoutly for what are mere accessories ? Why should the removal of certain ornaments from the altar be spoken of as desecration ? The truth is that deep down below what appears on the outside there lurks a secret feeling in every heart, amounting in sincere and earnest souls to an intense conviction, that these externals around which the contest turns are symbolic of doctrine ; that they point to something which is either truth revealed by God or errors invented by man; and that this doctrine, be it true or false, is of the highest importance. The one side believe that the bread and wine after the words of consecration become in some way or other nothing less than the Body and Blood of Jesus Christ, to which, since He is now impassible and immortal, are inseparably united His Soul and His Divinity; in other words, they believe, that Jesus Christ, God and Man, is present upon the altar under the appearance of bread and wine, demanding of course their highest homage and adoration. They contend, then, as for a matter of life and death, for all that betokens His presence, for the lights that symbolize the Light of the world, for the flowers that typify the essential beauty, for the vestments that mark the sacrificing priest, and so on. The other side believe, on the contrary, that the bread and wine remain after consecration nothing more than bread and wine, that the presence of Jesus Christ there is merely spiritual, and that there is no sacrifice offered up, because there is no victim. According to this belief, to adore what is on the altar would be idolatry of the grossest kind, and therefore whatever appears to lead to such adoration is very justly disliked. . . . The strife, then, when examined in its real and not in its apparent cause, is clearly no insignificant one. What the contending parties have at heart, although perchance they have it not on their lips, is simply truth. Each side is upholding what they consider to be Divine truth, and opposing what they consider to be the grossest error. It is truth they are seeking for, not on some minor point, but concerning the chief act of Christian worship. When the minister consecrates, is it God who is on the altar, or is it bread? What we receive into our mouths, is it bread and wine, or is it the Body and Blood of Jesus Christ, living with His Soul and adorable Divinity? This is in reality the question at issue between the two contending parties. Who can deny that it is one of the very highest importance, and one which ought to be decided without delay?

"But it is time to turn our attention to the Bishop of Brechin, the chief pastor of the contending parties, and examine the remedy he proposes for healing the strife. A superficial observer might not perceive the real question, but he who has been so long intimate with both sides must be thoroughly well aware that what they are endeavouring to maintain is the truth or untruth of a most important doctrine. . . . One would have supposed that his course as Bishop would have been perfectly simple and straightforward. One would have supposed that the Bishop would have promptly exercised his office, that he would have mounted his pulpit, and with all the authority which he claims in spiritual matters would have taught what was the truth, and what was not the truth, and that if after that any persons had been so bold as not to believe him, there would simply have been no more connection between them and Bishop Forbes and Bishop Forbes' churches. Very far, however, from settling the question in this straightforward and apostolic manner, he gives us to understand that it is not in his power. He does not know, and therefore cannot teach, what is truth and what is error on the matter. But we must allow him to speak for himself. ' I have to deal with a case,' he says, ' which brings before me the two extreme sections of the Church of England. The Church of England has always been comprehensive, and it is a matter of historical truth that, rightly or wrongly ' (he does not know which), ' there have existed in it two schools of thought since the time of the Reformation.' Two schools of thought! Rather delicate wording for the matter in hand ; one would suppose him to be speaking of some merely theoretical opinion, instead of one of the most tremendous mysteries of religion ; whichever way the truth lies, it must be a matter of faith and not a mere opinion. If it be true that every time the words of consecration are uttered God works so stupendous a miracle as to change the bread and wine into the Body and Blood of His only-begotten Son—if indeed God humbles Himself in so wonderful a degree as to give us His own Flesh to eat, and His own Blood to drink, then indeed to believe this undoubtingly must be a most necessary part of the faith of a Christian ; if it be not true, then to believe it and to act accordingly is the grossest superstition—nay, even the profoundest idolatry, and certainly does not deserve the gentle designation of 'a school of thought.' These two schools of thought, he goes on to explain, because the Church of England is so comprehensive, have been comprehended by her since the time of what he calls the Reformation ; and this means, when put into plain English, that persons who hold the doctrine of the Real Presence, and persons who reject it as error, have been included in her communion ; consequently, he as Bishop of this comprehensive Church, is bound to comprehend—that is, to include them too, so long at least as they are willing to be so comprehended. In other words, the Church of England either cannot or will not teach which is the truth or which the falsehood on this great subject, and as a consequence the Bishop of Brechin, as taught by that Church, does not know to this day the right or the wrong on the matter. Who can blame him, then, for not teaching it? It is his misfortune, not his fault. Having thus declared his inability to settle the question by teaching the truth, the good Bishop sets to work to adjust matters as best he may. 'I sanction,' he says, 'at the early service, at eight in the morning, such a form of worship as suits those who like an ornate religion ; at eleven I sanction a service in the plainer form.' One who had not considered the difficulties of the case would probably see something grotesque in this wonderful arrangement, but when one realizes the utter inability of the Bishop to settle the question in the right way, the wonder ceases. After all, he is only doing on a small scale what his Church has been doing ever since its existence. He is trying to comprehend or include within the walls of the same building, just as his Church has endeavoured to comprehend within the same communion, persons of two distinct and opposite beliefs. Alas ! to what straits has the comprehensiveness of his Church reduced him ! He is obliged to soften down the difference between two parties on an article of faith, and gently term them two schools of thought, or, more gently still, those who love an ornate religion, and those who like a service in a plainer form ; and the arrangement he has proposed to satisfy these two schools of thought comes to this : at one hour the service is to be ornate, there is to be a super-altar and vases of flowers ; at another hour these objectionable symbols are to be removed. At one hour there is to be a congregation engaged in adoring what they look on as God ; at another the very same substance is to be expressly treated as nothing more than bread and wine, and with perfect consistency everything that looks like homage is to be removed. . . Can this arrangement be considered as satisfactory ? Well, perhaps, if each of the congregation were as comprehensive in his views as the Bishop, it might. He can direct that at one service those things that are designed to signify the Real Presence and the Sacrifice of the Victim be there, at another that they may be removed. He can also, we presume, accommodate himself so far as to officiate now at the one service, which is expressly intended to honour what is on the altar as our Lord, now at another, which is expressly intended to treat it as bread and wine ; at one time, apparently at least, to adore it as God, at another to renounce that adoration as error and superstition ; for it cannot be forgotten that the retaining or removing these decorations are intended, by the congregation at least, as expressive of their acceptance or of their rejection of the doctrine of the Real Presence. . . . The remedy applied by the Bishop is by no means satisfactory, because it fails to touch the root of the evil. It is not to be wondered at, then, that a number of his flock, foreseeing doubtless the Bishop's power-lessness to aid them, should have kindly come to the rescue by proposing to take the matter into their own hands, and securing themselves on the one hand from a clergyman who would teach false doctrine, and on the other from ceremonies which would maintain it. . . . Had the Bishop been wise, he would have sheltered himself in his distress under this kindly offer ; but no—he reclaims on the score of infringement on his spiritual power, he requires obedience to his authority as pastor, quoting the words, " Obey them that bear rule over you," asserts that the management of the services is in the hands of the clergy by Divine authority, and warns his flock of the sin of schism into which he fears they are drifting.

"From this we gather that, although unable to forbid observances considered by many as idolatrous, or acts called by others desecrations, he yet claims submission to his decision on the ground of his divinely instituted authority, and condemns those who would separate themselves from him rather than submit, as guilty of the sin of schism. Since he raises his claims so high, it would be well to examine into their validity, and to inquire whether or no he has solid ground for the authority which he assumes. What is his authority, and where did he get it ? If he be indeed entrusted with so high an embassage, he should be able to show his credentials.

"The Bishop claims a spiritual authority over souls because he is a Bishop, and this is what all Episcopalians believe to belong to a Bishop by Divine appointment. Unfortunately, however, it must be admitted that it is very doubtful, to say the least, whether Dr. Forbes is a Bishop at all. Out of some thousands of persons now living who in different parts of the world bear the title of Bishop, not more than a mere handful would allow that he was one at all. Were the question put to each of them, Is Dr. Forbes a Bishop? an overwhelming

E

majority would answer, No, nor even a priest. This is at least quite sufficient to throw a very grave doubt upon his claims, and to make sensible people hesitate and inquire before they yield submission, more particularly as he has shown himself so utterly incapable of performing the most important part of a Bishop's office, which is to teach the truth, and to point out error. But even, supposing it granted, for argument's sake, that he is a Bishop, something would still be required to make good his claims. The mere fact of being a Bishop would not give him power over a single soul or over the services of a single church. He must have besides, as he well knows, what is called jurisdiction, that is, he must be empowered to exercise his spiritual authority over a certain territory, and over the souls contained in it. A Bishop cannot exercise his authority everywhere, but only within the limits which are assigned him by competent authority. Unless, then, he has received jurisdiction over the souls in Dundee, and received it, too, from an authority that has power to confer it, he has no more reason to claim the obedience of any persons in Dundee or to arrange any of the services in any church of Dundee, than has the Bishop of Pekin. Now, this spiritual jurisdiction can only be given by God, or by those on whom God has bestowed the power of conferring it, since God alone gave to man any authority in spiritual things over the souls of his fellow-men. The question then is—Has he who calls himself the Bishop of Brechin got spiritual jurisdiction over the souls within that territory? If he has, it must have been given him by competent authority; and if we ask him who gave it, he will doubtless answer—The Church of England in Scotland, or the Scotch Episcopalian Church with its Bishops. Has, then, the Scotch Episcopalian Church the power to give spiritual jurisdiction over the souls contained within the limits of what is called the diocese of Brechin? Such power was certainly never given to it, for there is no doubt of the fact that before the so-called Reformation the Church in Scotland received jurisdiction from the Bishop of Rome. Every Bishop had his power from that one centre of authority, which was believed to have received the supreme power from Jesus Christ Himself. If the question had then been asked: Where did the Bishop of Brechin get his jurisdiction, the answer would have been simple: From the See of St. Peter, that supreme centre of authority instituted by our Blessed Saviour. But the Church of England and the Church of

England in Scotland rebelled against this supreme authority, and therefore no longer received jurisdiction from it. Perhaps Bishop Forbes will answer: 'The Church of England in Scotland is independent, and able of itself to give jurisdiction,' but still the question remains without a satisfactory reply. How did it become independent? What makes a Church independent? Does it require a certain extent of ground, or a certain population, or a certain number of Bishops? Would four be enough, or three, or would one be enough to constitute a Church *sui juris* and possessing jurisdiction in itself? The truth is, the only way in which the said Bishops can account for their jurisdiction is by saying that they have assumed it; therefore it is not of Divine origin, and no one can be obliged to submit to it. So far indeed from being of Divine origin, it has its source in schism. Bishop Forbes deprecates the sin of schism, and yet he is actually a leader of schism, and whatever jurisdiction he claims was derived from that schism. Supposing, by way of illustration, that one part of his flock were to break away, get a Bishop consecrated somehow or other for themselves, and proceed to proclaim their independence as a separate Church, would not the Bishop cry out loudly against the sin of schism? Yet that is exactly what his predecessors did with regard to the Catholic Church. A part of the Church in this country broke away, and separated themselves from the rest of it, and threw aside their connection with the See of Rome, whence all their jurisdiction had proceeded, and proclaimed their own independence. What on earth was that but schism? If it be not, then schism is a word without meaning, for Bishop Forbes is still continuing the same schism in defiance of the Catholic Church, which has at this day a Bishop with real jurisdiction over the very territory where he claims it; and so Bishop, or rather plain Dr. Forbes, is considered and treated by the Catholic Church as a schismatic, just as he would consider one who separated from himself."

The state of affairs in my old congregation, after my departure from Dundee, is so excellently stated in this pamphlet, which bears the title of " *The Bishop of Brechin and his Flock ; or, The War in Blinshall Street* (the street in Dundee in which my Church of St. Mary Magdalene's was situated). By an Observer. Dundee, 1868 "—that I have not hesitated to incorporate selections from it in my " Recollections of Scottish

Episcopalianism." The circulation of this pamphlet, along with the step which I had taken, bore fruit in due time in conversion to the Catholic Church of many members of my old flock.

10.

To return to my more personal narrative, one excellent piece of advice was given to me by Dr. Manning. "The very best thing you can do," he said to me, "is to forget or to ignore all the Christianity you have ever learned, and to begin at the beginning, and have it *taught* to you, and learn it all up again as for the first time. It is like a man with a broken leg which has been badly set. He had much better have it broken again and then set properly. It may be painful, but it will be satisfactory." I acted on his advice.

By the same advice I went straight away to Rome, and there it was that I abandoned the study of St. Thomas. I went to Rome *to learn*, and to drink in, and at its source and from the bosom of the "Mother and Mistress of all Churches of the world," the religion of Jesus Christ. I went *in spiritû pupillari* to place myself *in statû pupillari*. Hence it was that I found myself free from all the difficulties which beset even Catholic Englishmen when they find themselves for the first time in Rome. These are not seldom apt to compare Roman usages, to which they have hitherto been strangers, with the usages with which they have been familiar throughout all their lives in England. True John Bulls, in their most honest bullheadedness—which is in an entirely different category from pigheadedness—they are inclined to weigh, to measure, and to value every Roman practice by the standard of the practices to which during all their lives, and from their childhood, they have been accustomed at home. In the narrowness of provincial minds home and Rome find themselves in contrast, if not in conflict.

From this home-sickness in the religious sphere I have never suffered. In Rome I found myself *at home*. I did not find anything there to scandalize me, as the English tourist, even if he is an English Catholic, is not seldom scandalized. All things that I saw on the surface of Catholic life in Rome combined to edify me, or build me up and solidify me in the Catholic and Roman faith. What most struck me in Rome was the devotion of the Roman *men* at the early Masses in the morning. They were praying *like women*. Devout men in England seem to be praying under protest. The Roman men were so simple and so unaffected in their devotions. Quite naturally they would on occasion interrupt their prayers to tell or hear a piece of news, or to give or take a pinch of snuff. As naturally they returned to their devotions, and placed themselves again, and in a way the reality of which no one could mistake, in presence of their Maker.

II.

My years of amateur study of St. Thomas ended when I came to Rome. I was now no longer to read for myself, and at my own discretion, but to listen to a living voice, and to learn in subjection to a master. The masters in the true Israel who were then teaching at the Jerusalem of earth, were mighty men, and men of renown. There were giants on the earth in those days. There was Ballerini, the prince of moral theologians, a man who has done more than has any other living man to mould the minds of the confessors of our time, and that throughout the world. Men of all races and of all countries were assembled in his class-room, and they have carried his maxims and his methods into every land. Some of his opinions in Moral Theology were not undisputed, but these opinions were not disputed by many, if by any, of his own disciples. He spoke as a man having authority, and the authority which he claimed was not that of his own genius or of his own learning, but the authority which sprang from the fact that he sat there teaching in the capital of Christendom, at the feet of the Vicar of Jesus Christ, with his doctrine well known, *urbi et orbi*, to the priesthood not only at the centre, but to the circumference of the Universal Church, and no man, however much he might dislike his opinions or dispute them, was able to secure an authoritative condemnation of them. Lecturing on a certain point, his view of which had been vehemently opposed by not a few even among the learned in moral science, he said to us one day : "They may try, when you get home, to bully you out of my doctrine, but don't let them do it. I will give you one plain and simple rule : 'What it is safe for me to teach, it is safe for you to practise.'" Ballerini *mortuus adhuc loquitur*—"being dead he yet speaketh," and that through Father Palmieri, who has edited Ballerini's magnificent posthumous work on Moral Theology. Of Palmieri also, as one of the two professors of Dogmatic Theology, I was a pupil. Outside Rome, Palmieri would have been in the first rank of living theologians, but in the Roman College there were living men who towered head and shoulders far above him, such as Father (afterwards Cardinal) Franzelin. It was as great a privilege to have been Franzelin's pupil as it would have been to be the pupil of Suarez, or Vasquez, or De Lugo. Franzelin and Palmieri were both of them among my examiners for the degrees of Bachelor and Licentiate of Theology in the Gregorian University of Rome.

I remember going one day, with some of my fellow-pupils, to visit Father Franzelin in his room. We told him, in expectation of his approbation, that we had been buying some books at the sale of a late Cardinal's effects, to form the nucleus of a theological library. " Library!" he cried, "what on earth do students want with a library? *Read my text.* I tell you what it is : If young men come here and spend here four years, and then take the *Laurea* (the degree of Doctor of Theology), and go away thinking themselves to be theologians, they have simply spent those four years in vain. All that the *Laurea* means is this—it is a certificate that *perhaps* they are then fit to be trusted with a book."

Father Franzelin's advice was sage and sound. I followed it, and have found the benefit of it. It is then only after one is in possession of a mental backbone, and a backbone that cannot be created in one's own mind by one's own efforts, but only through the influence of a living voice which is uttered by a recognized authority, that one can afford to clothe that backbone with the flesh of further knowledge derived from private reading. Philip said to the eunuch of great authority, the treasurer of Candace, the Queen of the Ethiopians, when he heard him reading in his chariot the book of the Prophet Isaias, " Thinkest thou that thou understandest what thou readest ? " The eunuch answered, " How can I, unless some one show me ? "

12.

There remains the problem : How was it possible for a man, who for some six years had been not only living immersed day by day in the study of St. Thomas, but had written and published Digests of St. Thomas' doctrine on the Incarnation and on the Sacraments, to have remained blind to the fact of the existence of the Catholic and Roman Church, as it is the one and only Church of Christ on earth.

One reason there is, and it is to be found in the fact that the highest idea in the Protestant mind of the position of the Roman Pontiff in the Catholic Church, is the idea of his being a sort of Metropolitan of the world. This is natural. The idea of the Catholic Church in a Protestant mind, is only an extension of the Protestant's idea of the Protestant's own communion. In that communion, the Archbishop of Canterbury holds the foremost place, and is the highest prelate. From that which he is to the Protestant Bishops and people of England, an Anglican not unnaturally takes his idea of what the Roman Pontiff is to the Catholic Bishops and to Catholic priests and laymen throughout the world. A Protestant can understand the Pontiff's claim to be Bishop of Bishops, in a sense similar to that in which an Archbishop is superior of the suffragans of his province. A Protestant can see certain advantages in the Pontiff's possessing a patriarchal pre-eminence over the Bishops and Archbishops of the world. It is possible for a Protestant to desire and long and pray fervently for the return of the Church of England to Catholic unity. The motive of his desire is the argument that the same reasons which require Episcopacy seem to demand the Papacy as its complement. A Bishop is seen to be necessary as a centre of unity to the clergy of a district. A Bishop of Bishops seems equally necessary as a centre of unity to the Bishops of the world. Without some such centre of unity, the Universal Church—understood as being the aggregate of all particular churches, whether national or diocesan—would clearly be destitute of a perfection which belongs to every particular Church or diocese. The Protestant, as a man who has come to use of reason, is well aware that every society, or every body of men, consists of head and members, and that a head is as necessary to the existence of a society or corporate body, as are the members themselves. He knows that without a head there cannot exist a real society, or a society in any true sense. He regards Christendom, therefore, as disintegrated. His dream is of a restoration of the unity of Christendom by means of the accomplishment of a scheme of a confederation of Churches. In this scheme, the Bishop of Rome would hold, and rightly, the central and the chief place. The Bishop of Rome would be the centre of unity to the Bishops of the world. He would have a pre-eminence of honour among his fellow-Bishops, and would preside in their assemblies or General Councils. Appeals might be made to him in the last resort. He might also take cognizance of abuses. He would, in short, be Patriarch of the world.

Such is the highest idea of the Catholic Church in the Protestant mind. It is not the idea of the Church of God. It is a human idea, and it is not the one Divine idea. It is beautiful because, so far as it goes, it is true. The Roman Pontiff is indeed all that the High Church Protestant would allow, or would have him to be, but he is also a great deal more. The Protestant fails to realize that the Roman Pontiff is not only Bishop of Bishops, but is Bishop also *omnium Christifidelium*, of all and of every one of Christ's faithful laity.

The Catholic faith teaches that the Roman Pontiff is in possession of *direct* and *immediate* ordinary jurisdiction over every baptized person. His jurisdiction over every Christian, man and woman, is *ordinary*, to use an ecclesiastical phrase— that is to say, jurisdiction belongs to him in virtue of his office, and he has power to delegate his jurisdiction. In other words, every Catholic lives in subjection to two Bishops. He is directly subject to the local prelate within whose diocese he has his dwelling. He is also as directly subject to the episcopal jurisdiction of that Universal Bishop — *cujus diocesis est orbis terrarum*—whose diocese is the world, or, in other words, is worldwide.

The Roman Pontiff is *Universal Bishop*. He is not indeed Universal Bishop in any sense which should imply that there exists no other Bishop upon earth, that he is the one and only Bishop, and that all others who are called by the name of Bishop are not real Bishops, but are only his vicars or his deputies. This is more than manifest, since it belongs to the Catholic faith, and to the profession of the Catholic faith, to teach and hold that every Bishop is a true prince within the limits of his own princedom. The Pontiff is *Universal Bishop* not merely in the sense that he is Bishop of Bishops, and that consequently every one of the faithful who is subject to his own local Bishop, must necessarily be *in a manner* subject to that Bishop's Superior. The Roman Pontiff is *Universal Bishop* in the sense that his episcopal jurisdiction is *universal*, and that he is *directly* and *immediately* as much the Bishop of every Christian layman as he is the Bishop of every Catholic Bishop. It is the birthright of every Christian to have right to have recourse to the Roman Pontiff *as to his own Bishop*. The

Pontiff is Supreme Pastor of all, both sheep and lambs, who are living on earth within the one fold of the one flock of God.

To the Protestant mind this may seem to create an *imperium in imperio*, and to result in a conflict of duties. "No man can serve two masters," and how—may a Protestant say—can any man be directly and immediately subject to two Bishops? This difficulty and objection is again the natural result of the Protestant conception, or misconception, or inadequate conception, of the Church of God. The Protestant conception stops short at a confederation of churches. The Catholic and Divine idea is that of one society—one organic body—one living and not only undivided but *indivisible* Church—which is subject to the supreme rule and government of one Universal Bishop. In this society there is not only union and communion of members one with another, but there is also due subordination of all the members to one common Head. Every member of the *one body* has not only place within that body, but has his own place. The head of the body has as clear a right to his own place in the body as have the members of the body to their place within the body. The mystical and visible Body of Christ upon this earth of ours is a Body which is organized and living. As such it must be one, and in its oneness it must be indivisible. The Bishops are the principal members of this visible Body. They have in it their place and their own place as members, and as principal members, but they nevertheless and in spite of their pre-eminence as principal members, remain members. They are not heads of that body. The mystical Body of Christ is as incapable of being hydra-headed as it is incapable of being headless. The Roman Pontiff is the one visible Head of the one visible Body, and there is, as there must be, an inflow of energy and action from the one Head upon all and every one of the members of that corporate society or body.

There is not, and there cannot be, any conflict of jurisdiction between the Head and the privileged members of the Body of Christ, which is His Church; that is to say, between the Pope, as Universal Bishop, and the local Bishops of particular churches or dioceses. This is a necessary consequence of the necessary subordination in every society of the individual and the particular to the general and the universal. It is by the Universal Bishop that the elections, by whomsoever they may have been made, of Bishops for particular dioceses are confirmed. It is by that Pontiff that those Bishops are instituted to their pastoral office and jurisdiction. This jurisdiction they exercise subject to the control of their Superior, who is supreme, and from their exercise of their episcopal office he has divine right and power at any moment, and at his discretion, to depose them for what he himself judges to be a lawful cause.

Further, if any country should be deprived at any time of all its diocesan Bishops, and even of all its priests, the Catholic Church in that country will not thereby have become extinct. It has not ceased to exist, and it still remains under episcopal rule and government. That country does not then *revert* to the Roman Pontiff. He does not then begin to assume for a time the episcopal supervision of it. It *remains* under his episcopal care as it was before it was deprived of its local Bishops. The Pontiff may, if it shall seem good to him, govern that afflicted country by means of Vicars Apostolic, and without the intervention of diocesan Bishops. So long as there remain in the country even only some Christian laymen, these men, as members together with their Head, the Roman Pontiff, constitute the body which is the Catholic Church in that country.

If, on the other hand, all the Bishops, priests, and laymen, in any country were, as one corporate body, to sever themselves from the rest of Christendom by renunciation of their allegiance to the Universal Bishop of the Universal Church, what would their position, or the position of that body, be? St. Paul has told us of the one Body with the one Spirit, which is the one mystical Body of Christ, as it is visible here upon the earth. This Body Jesus left behind Him when He ascended from earth to Heaven. It consisted of visible members who were many in number, and of a Head which was one in number. In this body all the members were disciples, while some were also Apostles. All were taught, while some were also teachers. The visible Head of all the members, of all the Apostles, as well as of all their disciples, was—one living man. Over all superiors, as over all inferiors, that one man was supreme. The mystical Body of Christ upon the earth is a visible kingdom, and it is the Kingdom of Christ upon the earth. It is a Divine monarchy, and as a monarchy it is and it must be ruled and governed by a *monarch*. As a *divine* monarchy, its reigning monarch must rule and govern by *divine right*, as chosen, called, anointed, crowned, and seated on his throne, not by his own will and action, or by the will and action of men, but by the will and action of all men's common Maker. The Vicar of Jesus Christ must be as divinely *sent* as was the Christ Himself. Jesus said to His Apostles—the men who were *sent men*, as distinguished from the men who were disciples, or *taught men*—"As My Father sent Me, so send I you. He that heareth you heareth Me." Addressing His Eternal Father, and with reference to His Apostles, Jesus said : "As Thou hast sent Me into the world, I also have sent them into the world. . . . And not for them only do I pray, but for those also who *through their word* shall believe in Me— that they all may be one, as Thou, Father, art in Me, and I in Thee, that they also may be one in us, that *the world may believe* that Thou hast *sent Me*."

That which St. Paul has told us about the one Body with the one Spirit, has consequences which our own divinely-given reason discerns and confirms. We see clearly, and so clearly, that we cannot believe or think it otherwise—that, once given that the Church of Christ was constituted by Christ after the manner of a living human body, oneness of corporeal being is a necessary property and an essential note of that one Church of the one Christ. (2) That in order to the living oneness of an organic structure, there must be a two-fold principle of oneness—an inward principle and an outward principle ; there must be one indwelling soul which informs the whole body and informs all and every one of the parts of the body, giving life to it and them, and binding them together in the oneness of one corporeal life. (3) And that, in order to this indwelling of the one life-giving soul there is required, as a necessary condition, the external oneness of the parts of the visible body, of the various members one with another, and of all of them with their common head. If the head of a living body were severed from the trunk of that body, the continued indwelling of the life-giving soul would be an impossibility. The whole body, head and members alike, would then undeniably be dead. If, on the other hand, a member, such as an arm or a foot, were to be severed from a living body, the body would not necessarily die, but in the severed member there would be no longer the one life-giving soul, and that member would therefore necessarily be destitute of life. In the Church of Christ, severance of the visible Head from all the members of the visible body is an absolute impossibility. The ever-abiding and ever-indwelling of the Holy Ghost—as the one Spirit in the one Body of Christ all days even to the consummation of the world—has been guaranteed by the promise of Christ Himself. The words of Jesus are equally a guarantee for the immortality of a visible Body, consisting of visible members in union with their visible Head. The continuity and the identity of that body are correlatives of the continuance of the Holy Ghost within it as its life-giving Spirit.

Suppose the existence of an amputated member or amputated members on the one hand, and the existence of the remaining members in union with their head, on the other hand, it is clear that the one life which was the result of the indwelling of the one life-giving soul, cannot possibly belong to both of the severed parts, and it is as clear that it cannot belong to the members which are headless.

The words of St. Paul—" one Body and one Spirit "—are an extension of the same idea which was contained in the words of Jesus Himself to His Apostles and disciples, " I am the Vine, you are the branches ; the branch cannot bear fruit of itself, unless it abide in the vine." The doctrine of the Apostle, as it is an extension of the doctrine of Him who sent him, cuts at the root of that branch theory which the Scottish Episcopalians, along with the High Church Anglicans, engrafted on the similitude of the Vine. The idea in their minds was that of living cuttings from a parent stem. This idea is rendered inconceivable when it is apprehended that that which is cut away is a member which is severed from a living body.

But why did we Scottish Episcopalians not see this, and why were some of us so long in discovering that which now seems to us to be so very elementary a truth ? We were ready to see our way into the Catholic and Roman Church. We longed to find a motive which would justify us in conscience in our desertion of the Episcopalian Church, both Scottish and Anglican—and nevertheless we could neither see our way nor discern any adequate motive for that which we would have given our eyes to do. Why did we not see the truth, which was there lying patent and evident before our eyes? The reason is not so very far to seek, and it is to be found imbedded in the doctrine of the Catholic faith. A visible thing is a proper object of the sense of bodily vision. To the eyes of the body in their normal and healthy state there belongs the power of vision of every visible thing which presents itself to their gaze.

One thing, however, can prevent the seeing of the visible object, however acute and penetrating may be the power of vision in the bodily eye. If that eye, along with the visible object, both find themselves in a place of darkness, the eye, with all its keen power of seeing, cannot see, and the visible object, whatever its obtrusiveness upon the eyesight, cannot possibly be seen. In order to see and to be seen, there must be *light*.

As it is in the natural order, so is it also in the supernatural order—there must be light. Light is a necessary condition in order to both the actual visibility of the visible and exercise of the power of vision. Whatever my faculty of vision may be, I cannot, so long as I am in darkness, see any object, however visible it may of its own nature be—there must be *light*.

There is the crucifix before me on my table as I write, and I see it because it is visible in itself, is within the sphere of my vision, and I have the faculty of sight, and the light is streaming through my window. But if this room, which contains me and that crucifix were in darkness, I should not see it, visible as it is in itself to eyes which have not only power of vision, but must see every visible object which presents itself to them to be seen. The case is exactly the same in the sphere of faith. There are the divinely revealed truths divinely made visible, and divinely presented to the minds of men—and there are those minds made by their Maker for recognition of truth, as it is the proper object of them, or that towards which they of their very nature tend, and in the attainment and possession of which they find the rest and peace of certainty—the "joy and peace of believing" for which they crave. And yet, and as matter of fact, we find that there are many and a multitude of men in this country of ours who, with all their sincerity, and in spite of all their efforts, do not discern those Divine truths which now seem to us so apparent and even evident. And why? Many of them have minds which are more capacious, and intellects which are more far-seeing, and a logical or reasoning power which is more acute and keen—and yet they do not see that which we have seen and see—and why?

What can the reason be? The reason was made plain to me during that Monday night and following morning in the train on my way from Dundee to London. In one moment, and it must be in one moment of time that a grace is given I got the grace. The light was shed into my soul; and I saw. I saw it then as clearly as I see it now. The Bride of Christ

—the one Catholic and Roman Church of God—arose in her beauty, and in the clearness of the light which her Heavenly Bridegroom gave me to behold her, every vestige of Anglicanism, or of Scottish Episcopalianism fled away as does the morning dew when the sun arises in his strength. From that moment to the present moment I have never had one disturbing doubt with regard to the claims of the Church of England, as by law established, or the claims of the Scottish Episcopalian Church, as by the same law disestablished.

The one as a branch or department, and perhaps the most important department of the civil service of this realm of England, I value, and even venerate. Towards the other I feel tenderly. For years she had flowing towards her the full tide of the whole and undivided devotion of a human life, but on that Monday night it was given me to see that the devotion was devotion to a bride of earth, and this devotion vanished like a mist in the light which gave me to behold the one Bride on earth of the one Bridegroom who is in Heaven.

These recollections of my past have risen up before my mind in the present of to-day, through a memory awakened by the sight of those two volumes which I found in a second-hand book-shop, and the authorship of which I was by the same memory compelled to recognize as mine. I have placed these volumes on the shelves in my room as monuments of a dead past, but side by side with other volumes which, begotten in Pentecostal light, are nevertheless and in some measure the offspring of studies which I made in darkness.

THOMAS BAKER,

1, SOHO SQUARE, LONDON.

Catholic Publications.

AGOSTINO DA MONTEFELTRO (O.S.F.), Conferences at Rome, Florence, and Milan, 1888—1891. Translated by C. AUBREY ANSELL and H. DALBY GALLI. 2 vols. Crown 8vo, cloth extra. 5s. net.

Only complete English edition.

CONTENTS.—Vol. I. Existence of God—Who God is—True Conception of Man—The Soul in Science and Art—The Immortality of the Soul—The End of Life and Religion—St. Joseph—Sorrow—The True Religion—Sources of Unbelief—The Working Classes—Mary. Vol. II. Jesus Christ—Christ the God Man—Doctrine of Jesus Christ —Purgatory—Love of Jesus—Our Faith—Hope—The Supernatural— Sunday Rest—Faith and Science—The Eucharist—Confession and Penance—Prejudice against Religion—The Passion, &c.

The only complete edition.

ST. JOHN OF THE CROSS, O.D.C. Complete works, *newly translated* from the Spanish, with a very full life of the Saint by DAVID LEWIS, 1888—1891. 2 thick vols. 8vo, cloth extra, £1 1s. nett.

LIFE OF DOM BARTHOLOMEW OF THE MARTYRS, O.P. *and Archbishop of Braga in Portugal.* Translated from the Biographies of Father Louis of Grenada and others by LADY HERBERT. In one thick vol. demy 8vo, cloth extra, 4s. nett.

ST. TERESA. BOOK OF THE FOUNDATIONS. Translated from the Spanish by the Rev. JOHN DALTON. Crown 8vo, cloth, 2s. 6d. nett.

ST. TERESA. WAY OF PERFECTION AND CONCEPTIONS OF DIVINE LOVE. Translated by the Rev. JOHN DALTON. Crown 8vo, cloth, 2s. 6d. nett.

ST. TERESA. THE INTERIOR CASTLE, OR THE MANSIONS. Translated by the Rev. JOHN DALTON. Crown 8vo, cloth. 2s. 6d. nett.

ST. TERESA'S LETTERS. Translated by the Rev. JOHN DALTON, with a *facsimile of the Saint's handwriting.* Crown 8vo, cloth, 2s. 6d. nett.

CARDINAL WISEMAN'S LECTURES ON THE PRINCIPAL DOCTRINES OF THE CATHOLIC CHURCH. (570 pp.) 1888. Crown 8vo, cloth extra, 3s. nett.

ANGLO-SAXON CHURCH. History and Antiquities of the Anglo-Saxon Church, containing an Account of its Origin, Government, Doctrines, Worship, Revenues, Clerical and Monastic Institutions. By Dr. JOHN LINGARD. New edition in 2 vols. crown 8vo, cloth extra, 5s. nett.

Two New Books by Father Humphrey, S.J.

CONSCIENCE AND LAW, OR THE PRINCIPLES OF HUMAN CONDUCT. Crown 8vo, cloth extra, 4s. 6d. nett.

RECOLLECTIONS OF SCOTTISH EPISCOPALIANISM. Reprinted from *The Month*, and revised by the Rev. WILLIAM HUMPHREY, S.J. (60 pp.) Royal 8vo, cloth extra, 2s. 6d. nett.

"A most interesting autobiographical account of the early clerical life of the author."

CARDINAL HOWARD. THE LIFE OF PHILIP THOMAS HOWARD, *Cardinal of Norfolk* (*b.* 1629, *d.* 1694), Grand Almoner to Catherine of Braganza and *Restorer of the English Province of Friar Preachers or* DOMINICANS, with a Sketch of the Rise, Mission, and Influence of that Order in England, by Father RAYMOND PALMER, O.P. 8vo, cloth extra, 2s. nett.

The history of Philip Howard of Norfolk is most interesting and useful, both as the story of a man who renounced rank, wealth, and position to become a simple friar-preacher, and also an account of the important part which he afterwards played in ecclesiastical affairs during the times of the last two Stuart Kings.

THE LIFE OF CARDINAL XIMINEZ (A.D. 1436—1517). By Dr. VON HEFELE *of Tubingen*. Translated from the German by the Rev. Canon DALTON, 1860. Thick 8vo, cloth, 3s. 6d. nett.

"A fine translation of the best life of the Great Cardinal, the Confessor of Isabella, the Founder of Alcala, and publisher of the Complutensian Bible."

THE BLESSED THOMAS MORE. A Dialogue of Comfort against Tribulation by Sir THOMAS MORE, Knight, *sometime Lord Chancellor of England*, which he wrote while prisoner in the Tower of London, A.D. 1534. 1891. Crown 8vo, cloth, 2s. nett.

"There is in these books so witty, pithy, and substantial matter for the easing, remedying, and patiently suffering of all manner of griefs and sorrows that may possibly encumber any man."

In the Press.

EXHORTATIONS ON THE CANTICLES. Translated from LOUIS DE PONTE, S.J.

THE ITINERARY OF THE SOUL TO GOD. Translated from ST. BONAVENTURA.

A HISTORY OF THE CATHOLIC CHURCH IN ENGLAND from the dawn of Christianity in this island to the re-establishment of the Catholic Hierarchy in 1850 (over 1200 pages). 2 thick vols. 8vo, cloth. Dolman, 1857 (published at 18s.). 5s. nett.

www.ingramcontent.com/pod-product-compliance
Lightning Source LLC
Chambersburg PA
CBHW021513090426
42739CB00007B/595